COUNTRY LIVING

FARMHOUSES

COUNTRY LIVING

FARMHOUSES

Stylish Decorating Ideas for the Classic American Home

MARIE PROELLER HUESTON

HEARST BOOKS
A division of Sterling Publishing Co., Inc.

New York / London
www.sterlingpublishing.com

Copyright © 2010 by Hearst Communications, Inc.

This book was previously published as a hardcover under the title *Farmhouses*.

Library of Congress Cataloging-in-Publication Data

Proeller Hueston, Marie.
   Farmhouses : stylish decorating ideas for the classic American home / Marie Proeller Hueston.
         p. cm.
   Includes index.
   1. Farmhouses--Decoration--United States. 2. Interior decoration--United States. I. Title.
NK2195.R87P76 2006
747'.886--dc22

                              2006006663

10 9 8 7 6 5 4 3 2 1

First Paperback Edition 2010
Published by Hearst Books
A division of Sterling Publishing Co., Inc.
387 Park Avenue South, New York, NY 10016

Book and jacket design by Gretchen Scoble Design

Country Living is a registered trademark of Hearst Communications, Inc.

www.countryliving.com

For information about custom editions, special sales, premium and corporate purchases, please contact Sterling Special Sales Department at 800-805-5489 or specialsales@sterlingpublishing.com.

Distributed in Canada by Sterling Publishing
c/o Canadian Manda Group, 165 Dufferin Street
Toronto, Ontario, Canada M6K 3H6

Distributed in Australia by Capricorn Link (Australia) Pty. Ltd.
P.O. Box 704, Windsor, NSW 2756 Australia

Manufactured in China

Sterling ISBN 978-1-58816-867-2

CONTENTS

FOREWORD

Of all the beautiful homes we've featured in *Country Living* over the years, it is often the farmhouses that are the most intriguing. There is a sense of quiet romance about these timeless structures. They are icons of American country style, combining classic details and casual comfort. Particularly fascinating are the many ways the interiors can be arranged to reflect the personal vision of the owners. Simply put, farmhouses look fabulous whether furnished with a few favorite pieces or brimming with collections, bathed in bright colors or painted all white, period perfect or filled with flea market finds.

You'll see all these looks and more in *Country Living Farmhouses*. There's a rambling Victorian in New York's Catskills region decorated with vintage linens, painted cupboards, and kitchen collectibles that recapture a mid-twentieth-century mood, an 1860s farmhouse in Vermont whose all-white interior is dotted with vibrantly colored textiles and home accessories designed by the owner, and a 1901 Georgia gem populated by creative groupings of prized possessions. Whether you live in the country or the city, this book will help you identify the looks you love so you can bring the romance of the American farmhouse into your home.

— The editors of *Country Living*

INTRODUCTION

Few images are as quintessentially American as a white clapboard farmhouse surrounded by gently rolling fields. Our enduring fondness for this form of architecture is twofold. Visually, we appreciate the structure's clean lines and simplicity of purpose. Emotionally, we respond to all that the dwelling symbolizes: our agrarian roots, our tenacity, and our resourcefulness as a nation. Far more than a dwelling place for a rural family, the farmhouse speaks to who we are as a people.

From humble shelters built by settlers to picturesque Victorian homes replete with wraparound porches and gingerbread trim, the evolution of the farmhouse in the United States parallels the territorial growth, ethnic makeup, and financial prosperity of the country itself. The earliest examples were constructed of rough-hewn logs set atop stone foundations—building materials that had quite literally been unearthed as colonists cleared the land for farming. Architectural elements varied by region. In New England, for instance, steeply pitched roofs discouraged the accumulation of snow. Further south, wide porches and thoughtful layouts brought cooling shade and cross ventilation. A community's traditions also played a role. The legacy of Dutch settlers can be seen in the stone farmhouses that dot the countryside of southern New York and northern New Jersey; Scandinavian immigrants in the upper Midwest adapted Old World log cabin construction to their new environs.

As the years passed, ideas and experiences regarding home building were shared with neighbors. Techniques that worked well were incorporated into new buildings while those that did not fell by the wayside. Eventually, a wholly American look began to take shape. Two of the most recognizable farmhouse styles from our pre-Revolutionary period hail from New England. One is the Cape Cod, which features a towering center chimney, steeply pitched roof, and symmetrical façade with two pairs of windows positioned on either side of a central door. The second style owes its creation to the tendency of growing families to build lean-to additions across the back of their houses. The distinctive rear roofline that resulted, one that sloped all the way down to cover the addition, inspired the structure's name, the saltbox. This mutable quality of the farmhouse—the ability to expand as a family grew and to reflect the changing tastes of each new generation—is one of its most enchanting traits.

The nineteenth century would prove to be the most influential time for American farmhouse design. For much of the first half of the century, an architectural style known as Greek Revival reigned supreme. Although the look originated in Europe, Greek Revival would reach its pinnacle of popularity in the United States as the young nation embraced the ideals of ancient Greek democracy. Identifying characteristics such as columns, pilasters, and pedimented windows adorned banks, municipal buildings, and domestic architecture both urban and rural. To mimic the look of the columned porticos that graced grand estates, country carpenters turned the gable ends of farmhouses toward the street, added pilasters to the corners, and painted the clapboard structures pure white.

As the century progressed, advancements in the mass production of building materials (lumber, nails, doors, and windows) found a vast market in the popularity of house plans that were broadly read in the new pattern books and periodicals. Add to this the fact that steamboats, railroads, and a bustling canal system helped farmers everywhere—even those in the most rural outposts—participate in the nation's growing prosperity and build themselves a handsome home in the prevalent style of the day. Italianate, Queen Anne, and especially Carpenter Gothic were popular Victorian styles that were transferred to farmhouse architecture. A simplified version of these pretty homes with welcoming front porches became the basic form that farmhouses took into the twentieth century.

Today, the American farmhouse continues to evolve, as homeowners pick up the torch and leave their own imprint on the residences of our forefathers and—mothers. Some people have accepted the challenge (and experienced the joys) of returning a centuries-old structure to its former grandeur, right down to the smallest period detail. Others decorate older farmhouses with a decidedly modern sensibility. And then there are those who build new homes that resemble the practical, pleasing silhouettes of yesteryear. Just as no two old farmhouses look exactly alike, each contemporary interpretation is unique.

Country Living Farmhouses celebrates this diversity of design and this connection to our nation's history. We've isolated six distinct approaches to farmhouse decorating: Sophistication, Colorful, Flea Market Style, Collections, Antiques, and New Homes. Throughout, you'll find information on the details that epitomize farmhouse style and how to re-create the look in your own home. Your personal vision might blend two of the categories listed above or perhaps incorporate a little from each one. No matter which style most closely resembles your own, you'll find endless inspiration on the pages ahead.

Chapter One

SOPHISTICATION

What constitutes a sophisticated take on farmhouse style? Quite often there is a pared-down feeling, a sparseness that is entirely intentional. Artwork and decorative details that are modern in appearance share shelf space with classic country antiques. Similarly, formal furniture and accessories that would otherwise look out of place in a rustic setting—a recamier, a high chest, an ornate wall sconce—are frequently paired with more casual pieces. Even within these confines, however, there is always room for personal interpretation, as the homes featured on the following pages artfully illustrate.

RETHINKING THE FARMHOUSE

Bull's-eye molding, paneled doors, and two-over-one windows are just a few of the original details that first attracted the owner of this circa 1900 dwelling in Bridgehampton, New York. Yet as much as the bones of the house spoke to him, the interior's small rooms proved inconvenient for frequent entertaining of family and friends. Updating the layout without sacrificing old-house charm was a challenge—but, in the end, the undertaking was a resounding success.

Among the owner's principal desires were more living space downstairs, a kitchen large enough and stylish enough to accommodate guests as dinner was prepared, and a master bedroom suite. An eighteen-foot deep two-story addition was built off the back of the house to increase the square footage while respecting the integrity of the exterior. On the bottom level of the addition, the home's original kitchen was merged with the new space to create a spacious den that spills out into a screen porch; the master bedroom was situated on the upper floor. Outside, cedar shingles were applied to the both old and new portions of the house, ensuring an even mellowing by the elements. Creating a sense of continuity between old and new was equally important indoors. To achieve this, a unified color scheme of warm cream and soft green was chosen and custom-made duplicates of original woodwork and windows were ordered. Furnishings throughout share a similar look: upholstered pieces in muted tones mingle with dark wood accessories. Underfoot, sisal rugs top deep-stained wood floors in each room. Simple white shades at the windows and carefully positioned, large-scale works of art on the walls underscore the interior's clean lines.

The home's elegant ease is evident as soon as you cross the threshold. The foyer's cream walls and crisp white woodwork are punctuated by a sunny ocher stair runner and the banister's dramatic silhouette. A doorway to the kitchen (formerly a library) was sealed off to redirect foot traffic through the living room, where pleasing shades of sage green, wheat, and berry-red evoke visions of harvest time. Placed in a wide circle, the living room's plush love seat and two comfortable armchairs invite relaxed conversation. Decorative details include lacquered boxes and a large portrait in a gilded frame. A wide band of white tops the walls above the windows to emphasize the intimate feeling of the space.

ABOVE: Soft, sun-washed colors—primarily creams and pale greens trimmed with white—appear throughout the house and create a sense of openness. In the living room, the white band around the tops of the walls makes the ceiling appear higher. Placed in wide circle, the living room's plush love seat and two comfortable armchairs invite a relaxed gathering.

OPPOSITE (top): Just off the living room is the dining room, where a similar wall treatment—soft green crowned by a band of white—unifies the two spaces. Chairs around the long, dark wood dining table are upholstered in a wheat-colored fabric.

OPPOSITE (bottom): The den is located in the home's new addition. The cream paint on the walls is the same shade as the foyer, visually connecting the two spaces. The screened-in porch is new, and is accessible through three sets of French doors. The wide stone slabs around the fireplace exude a contemporary look; fittingly, a piece of modern art was chosen to hang up above.

ABOVE: The owner's master bedroom is on the upper level of the new addition. Set against the taupe walls, the room's vaulted, four-point ceiling creates the illusion of a canopy above the bed. Heirloom furniture, including a chest of drawers, armchair, and love seat that once belonged to the owner's parents, helps tie the new room to the rest of the home's décor. Fabric with a subtle botanical print was chosen to reupholster the love seat and to make the bed's duvet and shams.

A CLOSER LOOK

LIGHTING
Located in the home's original library, the kitchen was a dim room that lacked sunny windows. Skylights were added to bring light into the space. The pendant lights over the work island are at once old-fashioned and slightly modern in appearance.

DETAILS
Wide beaded-board panels and traditionally styled knobs and half-moon pulls impart a rustic look to the new cabinets. The island's white surface calls to mind the marble-topped pastry tables common in nineteenth-century kitchens.

ISLAND
The work island was built as large as possible to accommodate not just cooks and their helpers but also guests, who are encouraged to pull up a bar stool and chat. An open shelf down below provides additional storage for cookware and serving pieces.

APPLIANCES
The range and ovens are made of stainless steel, but their finish is more subdued and their lines more rounded than many modern appliances. The blender, mixer, teakettle, and television are all color-coordinated to blend into the space.

COLLECTIONS
Dark, graphic objects such as game boards, tramp art frames, and wire baskets stand out against the room's light backdrop. Some of the pieces have a practical side as well: Wire baskets are ideal for storing onions, apples, and the like.

AN ABIDING LOVE

Our forebears were a resourceful lot. Whether building walls from stones unearthed with a plow or stitching patchwork quilts from clothing remnants, they made the most of the materials at hand. When decorating her Bucks County, Pennsylvania, farmhouse, one interior designer paid homage to our industrious ancestors. Each room incorporates an object or two that has been reused, recycled, or reimagined—a decorative box embellished with old buttons, a vintage rowing-club trophy wired as a lamp, and so on.

To create a neutral backdrop, wall and floor treatments are the same throughout much of the house. In the main living areas, putty-hued woodwork trims walls that have been plastered to attain a rustic appearance; creamy white paint coats both walls and woodwork in the kitchen and bedrooms. New heart-pine floors are unstained; in rooms that are carpeted, durable sea grass was chosen to stand up to frequent foot traffic by family, friends, and pets. Stairs ascend without banisters; the owner removed the originals with the intention of replacing them but found she preferred the resulting look. Sheer white shades dress the windows in the public areas of the house; simple curtains in subdued colors provide privacy in the bedrooms. The furniture is a mixture of everyday pieces that have traveled with her from previous residences and favorite finds from antiques shops, flea markets, and country auctions.

In the living room, for instance, a boxy armchair the owner found at auction years ago and reupholstered in wool is positioned beside an antique mantel installed to give the new fireplace the feeling of having always been there. To one side of the armchair, a shellacked log that the owner found for $5 supports a stack of books. In the dining room, a rough-cut cedar pedestal table stands at the center. Never a fan of matched sets of dining chairs, the owner instead brought together designs with distinct personalities such as Queen Anne, country Chippendale, and an old school bench made cozy with throw pillows and a graphic gingham blanket. In the kitchen, mismatched pendant lights—one in glass wrapped with a scarf and the other with an oversized fabric shade. Behind every decorating decision in these rooms and elsewhere in the house, the homeowner adhered to her philosophy of "use what you have."

ABOVE: The dining table is made of rough-cut cedar. Around it, seating in a variety of styles makes an energetic arrangement. The wrought-iron Medieval-style chandelier, designed by the homeowner, is a flat surface on which more than a dozen pillar candles have been configured.

OPPOSITE: A cooktop, ample counter space, and roomy storage shelves behind soft-green cabinet doors enhance the kitchen's large work island. The barstools are covered in a wheat-colored fabric. Pot racks mounted on the wall keep cookware close at hand and lend the utilitarian pieces a somewhat artistic flair. Open shelves set into the wall by the bank of windows showcase a collection of vintage ceramic vases.

ABOVE: The olive-green leather sofas have been in the owner's possession for decades. The wall directly behind one of the sofas was bumped out to make room for floor-to-ceiling windows that flood the room with light. Notice the prominently placed artwork in the room: Large-format photographs above the mantel and sofa are modern in feel, yet their rural subject matter makes them look right at home in this setting.

OPPOSITE: An ottoman serves both as footrest and additional seating in the living room. Its fabric picks up the olive green color of the leather sofas. The fireplace is new to the house, but the well-patinaed surround was purchased "as is" at auction.

ABOVE: A new balcony, accessible through glass doors, brightens the master bedroom. Behind the bed, a six-panel screen upholstered in damask stands as a unique headboard; all but one of the panels are attached to the wall. Simple draperies were fashioned from unlined linen in pale blue and charcoal gray. The seam where the drapery colors meet the folding screen creates a visual line that goes all around the room.

FARMHOUSE FAVORITE: DECORATIVE STENCILS

Wall stencils are an easy way to instill country charm in any room of the house. In early America, the practice was an inexpensive way for people of modest means to imitate the look of wallpaper in well-to-do homes. Then as now, the range of available patterns is broad: flowers, fruits, figures, vines, and swags are just a few of the motifs that can be found. Large designs can cover an entire wall, while decorative borders may be used to trim the top of a wall, the space directly above wainscoting, or the perimeter of a window frame. Consult how-to volumes in the library or bookstore to learn more about the process. Never been handy with a paintbrush? Check the yellow pages or inquire at a local historical society to find professional painters specializing in faux finishes.

A NEW LOOK FOR AN OLD HOUSE

For many of us, the décor of each room in our house is influenced by a single design style—traditional American country, for example, or mid-century modern. The owner of this Long Island, New York, farmhouse took a decidedly different approach. Her nineteenth-century charmer is a showcase for all her favorite looks, from the living room's elegant neoclassical formality to the master bedroom's Caribbean cool.

Letting each room speak to her, she tailored her choices for wall and window treatments, floor covering, furniture, and accessories to create unique interiors. The inspiration for the living room's neoclassical motif came from the mantel's intricate carving; the den exudes a more casual feeling that is well suited to its role as the family's destination for reading, writing, and playing games; country cottage is one way to describe the sunroom; and in the master bedroom, the owner wanted to capture the feeling of a visit to a Caribbean island.

Common design threads are woven throughout the house, ensuring that the eclectic mix works together as a whole. To begin, a neutral palette of creams and soft browns provides a cohesive look from one room to the next. Furnishings—whether elegant antiques or comfortable contemporary pieces—all possess an old-fashioned feeling. Finally, artistic touches personalize each interior: a repurposed coffee table, a graphic floor pattern, a single tapered candlestick set on a mantel, and fresh flowers arranged in unexpected vessels like urns, pitchers, teacups, and silver mint julep tumblers. The owner's eye for detail extends even out of doors to the front porch, where shuttered French doors complement the wrought-iron railing and stand out against the home's pale-yellow vertical clapboards. During the summer months, colorful annuals encircle a miniature, potted evergreen, adding an extra hint of color to the entrance.

A CLOSER LOOK

MANTEL
The mantel's ornate carving inspired the living room's neoclassical motif. To create a simple yet eye-catching arrangement, a single sculptural object was placed in the center of the mantel and flanked by topiaries.

STENCILS
A series of six-point stars was stenciled along the top of the wall all around the room. Choosing the same off-white paint for the stars that was used to coat the main portion of the walls ensures a subtle effect.

SEATING
Pairs of settees, armchairs, and love seats achieve a symmetrical look within the room while providing ample seating for family and friends. Upholstered in white muslin, a curved recamier shows off its silhouette.

COFFEE TABLE
Corinthian capitals discovered at auction stand in for a traditional coffee table. Positioning the intricately carved pieces on a diagonal visually diminishes the wide space between the love seats.

ARTWORK
Hanging a series of framed images in a grid pattern is a simple solution for empty wall space. Here, vintage prints of the White House in thin gold frames were chosen to complement the décor of the room.

ABOVE: Located in the former dining room, the den exudes a more casual feeling that is well suited to its role as the family's destination for reading, writing, and playing games. Wallpaper reminiscent of the stencil work of early-twentieth-century itinerant artist, Moses Eaton sets the mood. To prevent the busy pattern from overwhelming the space, whitewashed wainscoting was installed. Roman shades and a velvety sofa bring out the softer shades of the wallpaper, while a stained checkerboard floor pattern picks up the darker hue underfoot. Accessories such as a pine English pond yacht and ottomans covered in white-work quilts underscore the relaxed atmosphere.

ABOVE: Sand-textured cocoa walls, hand-stenciled palm trees, and a caned rosewood bench at the foot of the bed bring tropical flair to the dormered space. Above the mantel, a framed fabric remnant and a nautical print continue the theme. Classic country details include the Federal bell-and-ball tiger-maple four-poster, the floral-print quilts, and the energetic mix of red-and-white ginghams, stripes, and checks.

OPPOSITE: In the sunroom an overstuffed love seat beckons family and friends to rest awhile. Delightful details abound, from the throw pillows covered in vintage fabrics to the latticework carpet on the floor. Collections further personalize the space: Barn-wood birdhouses hang in front of the window, and a trio of teapots parades along a high shelf.

FAMILY HISTORY

When the family that owns this sprawling five-bedroom farmhouse in Watermill, New York, purchased the property in 1987, the house had been occupied by descendants of the original inhabitants for more than a century. This is a rarity. More often than not, old homes have gone through a succession of owners who each put their own stamp on the residence by means of renovations, additions, and updates. The current owners strove to respect the integrity of the woodwork, floorboards, and other distinctive features that had been left untouched while still making their new home reflect their own tastes.

A palette of bright white was chosen as a neutral backdrop throughout the house to make heirloom furnishings as well as treasures discovered in the farmhouse basement stand out. Walls, woodwork, and floors were painted white; the paint on the wide-plank pine floorboards has gradually worn away with each passing year to reveal the natural grain of the wood and attest to a new chapter in the history of the house. Aside from the occasional map or large-scale wall-hanging (such as a quilt or an American flag), walls are left bare. Fresh flowers, throw pillows, graphic antique quilts, and other accent pieces provide bursts of color in each room. Texture comes in the form of worn wooden surfaces and intriguing arrangements like stacks of art books set on a humble garden bench.

White slipcovers on the living room sofas enhance the overall decorating theme. To create a focal point in the room, the home's original mantel was stripped to reveal honey-colored pine; above it, a simple, wood-framed mirror makes a graphic statement on the wall.

ABOVE: White slipcovers on the living room sofas reinforce the overall decorating theme. The covers of the throw pillows are changed when the mood strikes: Bold hues complement flowers picked from the garden, faded floral prints achieve a more subdued effect, and velvet shams in deep jewel tones impart a festive, wintery feeling around the holidays.

RIGHT: The home's original mantel, the focal point of the living room, was stripped to reveal honey-colored pine; above it, a simple, wood-framed mirror makes a graphic statement on the wall. As with the living room's throw pillows, floral arrangements in the ironstone vase vary with the seasons from budding pussy willows in the springtime, cheerful sunflowers in the summer, delicate bittersweet in the fall, to fragrant greenery in the winter.

LEFT: Beneath the sunroom windows, a well-worn bench serves as a bookshelf for a collection of art books. A quirky map of Long Island hangs between the windows.

ABOVE: The two tables in the kitchen were discovered the basement of the house. An old table base was hauled upstairs and topped with butcher block to create a work island, while a small enamel-topped design was left as it was found. New red-and-white plaid seat covers grace a pair of metal garden chairs found at a local yard sale. Period details around the room include tongue-and-groove paneling and glass-front cabinets. In one corner, Polaroid pictures hung in a tight grid pattern form an artistic interpretation of the family photo wall.

ABOVE: The dining room chairs were discovered in the basement storage unit of their old apartment building. The French country dining table was moved with the family when they relocated to the house from their apartment in New York City.

ABOVE: In the guest bedroom, the iron bed is painted in a pale hue to maintain the room's open feeling. Pared down, the room still exudes a comfortable feeling with the colorful quilts and plump pillows.

FARMHOUSE FAVORITE: IRON BED FRAMES

As a staple in farmhouse bedrooms as far back as the nineteenth century, wrought-iron bed frames have never lost their appeal. Today, lovers of the style have two options for finding their favorites: they can shop for new frames at furniture stores and through mail-order sources, or they can search for vintage examples at flea markets, antiques malls, and country auctions. While the old models often exhibit the worn painted surfaces that many people appreciate, new frames can be ordered in queen and king sizes. (Most antiques are twin size or three-quarter size.) New beds can also be ordered in pairs if a matching set for a guest or child's room is desired. The variety of styles in both new and old frames, from simple to ornate, ensures that there is something on the market to suit every taste.

FARMHOUSE FORMAL

Farmhouses often grew with the families who occupied them, supporting extensions and additions as the need arose. In some cases, the line between newer and older portions of the house is imperceptible; in others, quite the opposite is true. For instance, this Bucks County, Pennsylvania, farmhouse is composed of two parts built a century apart: one in the late 1700s, the other in the 1880s. When the owners noticed incongruities between the flooring, windows, doors, and other details in the two spaces, they set out to create a more cohesive look. Salvaged molding, windowpanes, and wide-plank pine floorboards got the ball rolling. The couple's distinctive decorating style—blending her Norwegian heritage with his American roots—completed the job.

The interplay of American and European antiques is evident throughout the house. In the upstairs sitting room, a settee made in eighteenth-century France and slipcovered in muslin lives with an American farm table from the late-1800s that is painted blue. Used more frequently for entertaining than its second-story counterpart, the downstairs sitting room is more formal in feeling. Although even here rustic furnishings intermingle with more refined designs.

The dining room's décor is further evidence that formal European furniture and textiles can live compatibly within a traditional American farmhouse. The deep tones of the wood are softened with rich textiles, from the Oriental rugs on the floor to the antique silk valances and contemporary silk curtains that frame the tall 12-over-12 windows. The table is a composite antique: a seventeenth-century English base with a nineteenth-century top. The chairs, with their tapestry-style upholstery and nail-head trim, are twentieth-century reproductions of late-1700s French examples.

From Early-American pottery to still-life paintings to Victorian inkwells, cherished collections add to the home's wonderfully layered effect. The owners' love of one-of-a-kind objects extends even to their twenty-five-acre property where cement lions, decorative iron gates, and an ancient bronze ship bell populate verdant garden "rooms."

ABOVE: In the downstairs sitting room, artwork on the walls is arranged in the manner of the grand salons of Europe. Striped valances above the French doors complement butter-yellow walls trimmed with soft gray woodwork. Between the doors, an American breakfast table from the late 1700s is flanked by two side chairs with decoratively pierced backs. The Oriental rug supplies rich beauty and color underfoot.

OPPOSITE: The dining room demonstrates how formal European furniture and textiles can coexist within a traditional American farmhouse. A late seventeenth-century walnut cabinet stands between the windows, while the dining table is a combination of eras: a seventeenth-century base with a nineteenth century top. The side chairs are twentieth-century reproductions. The plaster-over-stone walls are stenciled with an intricate pattern.

OPPOSITE: No part of the American farmhouse cries for revival more than the practical mudroom. In this example, tiles of terra-cotta bring beauty to the mudroom floor which is more commonly laid with only the most humble boards. The owners designed the wide, Shaker-style hutch, painting it in pale-yellow to complement collections of yellowware bowls and blue-and-white stoneware crocks. A row of slippers in front of the hutch is a nod to the Norwegian custom of taking one's shoes off before entering the house; an 1850s American cupboard keeps shoes tucked away when not in use.

ABOVE: Heirloom and vintage textiles establish a sense of cozy comfort in a guest bedroom. Though small, the room is chock full of loving details, like a checkerboard floor pattern, delicate valances, and a faux-marble finish on the crown molding.

Chapter Two

COLORFUL

THERE ARE AS MANY WAYS TO BRING COLOR INTO A FARMHOUSE INTERIOR AS THERE

ARE HUES IN THE WORLD. WALLS, FLOORS, WINDOWS, FURNITURE, FABRICS, AND

DECORATIVE ACCESSORIES CAN ALL BE USED AS VEHICLES TO INTRODUCE VIBRANCY

INTO A ROOM. IN THIS CHAPTER, WE'LL VISIT FOUR HOMES, EACH UNIQUE IN ITS

APPROACH TO COLOR. IN ONE DWELLING, WALLS ARE COATED IN BOLD SHADES

INSPIRED BY GARDEN FLOWERS: MARIGOLD, POPPY, AND CORNFLOWER BLUE. IN

ANOTHER, WHITE WALLS FORM A NEUTRAL BACKDROP ONTO WHICH BRIGHT

FURNISHINGS ARE PLACED. SATURATED EARTH TONES SUCH AS OLIVE GREEN, SAF-

FRON, AND SIENNA ARE PLAYFULLY POSITIONED IN ONE PENNSYLVANIA FARMHOUSE,

WHILE A DOMINANT SCHEME OF RED AND WHITE PERSONALIZES A RESIDENCE IN

NEW YORK'S HUDSON RIVER VALLEY.

LIVING COLOR

Just as writers rely on words, the owner of this nineteenth-century New Hampshire farm-house uses color to express herself. Her bold brushstroke can be seen throughout the house from the entryway to the sleep chambers. Not only does the eye-catching palette lift her family's spirits during long New England winters, it also acts as a unifying force, allowing disparate furnishings (formal and informal, old and new) to coexist peacefully.

Stepping through the front door, guests are enveloped in marigold—a warm yellow-orange hue that flows from the hallway into the dining room. A light wash of reddish-brown brings texture to the dining room walls and conjures images of the tinted plaster walls of old European villas. Berry-red paint coats the interior of a built-in, glass-front cupboard, causing the silver tea sets stored inside to seem even more lustrous. A touch of red can also be found in the silk fabric that hangs at the window, forming light-catching drapes. Black accents around the room such as the upholstery fabric on the dining chairs, the shades on the wall sconces, and the thick frames on the artwork have a grounding effect on the overall scheme.

Poppy-red paint sets the tone in the living room. The vibrant shade coats walls as well as the back of bookshelves, making the volumes and artwork arranged there really stand out. To heighten the space's cheerful atmosphere, all woodwork is painted a crisp, glossy white, brightening the space. Upholstery fabrics inject small amounts of golden yellow and moss green into the room, while an Oriental carpet adds deep reds and blues underfoot.

The bedrooms share the same color preferences as the public rooms, and the children's rooms are especially lively. Although the bedrooms for grownups are somewhat more subdued, bold colors still play a major role in their décor. White walls in the master bedroom are energized by red woodwork around the windows and red molding at floor level. Vintage fabric in a floral print was fashioned into curtains. Painted turquoise and strawberry-red by the owner, the bed frame acts as the room's focal point.

ABOVE: Built-in storage was a staple of early farm-houses. Initially it was simply a practicality but later became more stylish (yet still functional). The built-in cupboard in the dining room is a typical example: an open display case above and closed storage below. The warm hues of the walls and trim glow in candlelight.

ABOVE: In the living room, a marble-topped coffee table and a comfortable sofa with white slipcovers act like the white woodwork, balancing the bolder hues of other furnishings. Color and pattern, family heirlooms and thrift-store finds mix easily to create an elegant room.

PAGE 54: The eighteenth-century desk in the living room is inlaid with a Dutch cityscape. It was found at an antiques market by the one of the homeowners' grandmothers.

PAGE 55: The airiness of the room's white walls and high ceiling is punctuated with bright splashes of color. The low-post bed is handmade and painted with colors that appear throughout the room in the trim, drapes, and folded quilt.

WARMTH AND WHIMSY

For a textile designer specializing in bright patterned pillows, hand-tufted rugs, appliqué coverlets, and painted bed linens, a house can become a calling card of sorts. Such is the case for the owner of this renovated farmhouse in Vermont from the 1860s. Her imaginative creations are showcased throughout the dwelling, creating a rainbow in every room. Walls in much of the house are white, so the bold accents pack even more of a visual punch. It was during an extended stay in Sweden that the owner honed her eye for color as well as her flair for interior design. It is a time-tested theory in Scandinavian countries that using lighthearted hues indoors helps alleviate the pall of long, dark winters.

In the living room, the walls and furnishings wear creamy coats of white, making accents like the sherbet-hued pillows all the more impressive. The owner's secret for successfully combining pillows of varying colors and motifs? Stick to the same intensity of tone and choose patterns that relate in scale.

In the kitchen, three walls of windows flood the room with light. The double-hung windows are shutterless and unadorned to capture every glimmer of sunshine winter has to offer. In warmer weather the windows frame a panoramic view of rolling hills and verdant fields. A corner hearth trimmed with tiles in animal motifs calls to mind the tiled stoves common in Swedish homes. A cozy reading area was created near the hearth by placing a love seat in front of the window and utilizing the windowsill as a bookshelf. Decorative finishes adorn the dining table and the circular side table, while a rug reminiscent of a Matisse painting covers floorboards that have been painted pale green. Collections of colorful glass and wire utensils share a similar sense of whimsy with the room's furnishings.

Shades of sea and sky were chosen for bedrooms and baths. Hand-painted duvets, sheets, and pillowcases designed by the owner are another distinctive feature of the bedrooms. A luxurious master bath is at once thoroughly modern and rooted in the past: beaded-board paneling sheaths the ceiling and walls as well as the platform of a deep tub fitted with an old-fashioned faucet.

OPPOSITE: In the living room, garnet and ruby-red fabrics adorn the seat of an elegant side chair and the plush ottoman that serves as a coffee table. The colorful pillows work together successfully because they have the same intensity of tone and the patterns relate in scale. On the floor, a graphic rug in more subdued shades adds texture to the scene without detracting attention from the colors elsewhere in the room.

ABOVE: In the large eat-in kitchen, double-hung windows are kept bare in order to capture every glimmer of winter sunshine. The white walls and pale green floor reflect the light. The painted table was handcrafted by a family friend.

OPPOSITE: A narrow strip of deep plum paint separates the paneling on the wall and ceiling; soft sky blue was chosen for the tub surround. The owner painted the wood floor's checkerboard pattern free-hand. Ceramic tiles in muted shades of blue and green add a grid pattern behind the tub. A single weathered side chair stands in front of the window, ready to support towels, bathrobes, or magazines in style.

ABOVE: The cozy guest room is painted in a soothing aqua-toned paint, perfect for displaying artwork against. Dowels on brackets hold curtains for guests' privacy; when no guests are visiting the homeowner prefers bare windows. The bedding was hand-painted.

DESIGNING WOMAN

Inspiration for an interior palette can come from many places—fall foliage, for instance, or a favorite fabric swatch. The owner of this 1830s farmhouse became captivated by Mediterranean hues during her travels in Italy, Portugal, and Spain. To transport a bit of sun-soaked European flair back home to northeastern Pennsylvania, she chose solid, deeply saturated shades of olive green, ocean blue, sunflower, and sienna for every room in the house. Sturdy wooden furniture pairs well with the strong color scheme. Decorative details are kept to a minimum, reflecting the owner's belief that less is more. Small doses of pattern and texture are introduced through rugs, table runners, curtains, upholstery, and bedding.

A medley of tints from the owner's favorite color family, green, distinguishes the foyer. Olive green coats the walls while a wonderfully tactile moss green fabric covers a wing chair. A wall of white behind the staircase and vintage barkcloth curtains at the window keep the dark walls from feeling oppressive. Woodwork in the dining room, situated just off the foyer, wears glossy nutmeg paint; a muted sky blue adds an unexpected touch of color to the ceiling.

The den's sienna walls call to mind weathered building façades along narrow Tuscan streets. Woodwork around the windows was stripped to accentuate the room's rustic feeling. A sofa and armchair set is upholstered in off-white; the color scheme of the furniture and walls is mirrored in the botanical motif of the carpet.

Saffron yellow sets the tone in the kitchen, a bright, spacious spot where the family gathers not only to eat, but also to read and work on creative projects. The beaded-board paneling and half-moon drawer pulls help the custom cabinetry achieve an old-fashioned look that is right at home with a set of wooden chairs. The floor's checkerboard linoleum pattern coordinates with the cabinetry and the hunter green countertops up above.

In the master bedroom, a color scheme of chocolate brown and teal create a comforting atmosphere. The walls are unadorned aside from a large circular mirror that rests atop an oak dresser. Roomy dressers and armoires were essential pieces in the farmhouse bedroom of long ago. The room's diminutive wallpaper pattern looks as though it could have popped right off of a vintage floral-print dress, proving once again that inspiration for home décor can be found in unexpected places.

ABOVE: A graphic green garden trellis displayed against the wall like a work of art complements the foyer's olive green walls that are visible through the doorway. A charming country-style chandelier provides a perfect finishing touch overhead. The homeowner painted the dining-room trim three times to achieve just the right shade of nutmeg.

OPPOSITE: In the kitchen, the saffron-colored walls were inspired by a trip to Spain. The back interiors of the glass-front cabinets were painted yellow as well to make the contents of the shelves look even better. Nicely revived with a fresh coat of white paint, the chairs were found at the Salvation Army.

OPPOSITE: Quilted blankets in pleasing shades of eggplant and chartreuse are kept on hand to drape over the back of the sofa or pile on the floor for additional seating. Brackets on the wall accommodate two guitars used for at-home music lessons. Displayed in such a manner, the musical duo makes an artistic statement as well as a practical one.

ABOVE: Blue-green walls dominate the master bedroom. A roomy dresser makes up for the typical lack of closet space found in farmhouses. A vintage blue plaid throw and a quilted cocoa bedspread and pillow sham set dress the bed and an old ladder doubles as a useful rack for blankets and clothing.

When the owners of a former dairy farm in New York's Hudson River Valley decided to build a new home, they turned the property's old farmhouse into comfortable accommodations for overnight guests. The dwelling's red exterior paint served as the inspiration for the color scheme inside: every room except the master bedroom is decorated with creative combinations of red-and-white furniture, fabrics, and accessories. The result is a lively mixture of old and new, patterned and plain.

In the open living-dining area, walls and woodwork (including the exposed beams) were painted a creamy shade of white. The living area sits beneath a vaulted ceiling and is spacious enough to accommodate a trio of sofas positioned around a square coffee table. The wide hearth dominates a reading nook in a corner of the room with a low ceiling. A set of four wooden side chairs and a pair of slipcovered chairs surround a long, French-style dining table.

A cozy bedroom tucked beneath the eaves illustrates another interpretation of the red-and-white theme. The pillows, sheets, duvet, and quilts combine floral patterns, checks, stripes, and stars to dress an iron bed frame. The shade of a standing lamp beside the bed was fashioned from the same large gingham fabric as a throw pillow. Because the bedding is all variations of red and white, any blanket or pillow carried to the living area will look right at home. To emphasize the simplicity of the space, the bedside table supports only an old-fashioned alarm clock and a black wire basket filled with imitation apples.

An outdoor "room," namely a small porch with panoramic views, is also done up in colors that coordinate with the overall decorating scheme. A red picnic table and red wooden benches complement the barn-red exterior wall of the house. Red-and-white quilts are draped over the table during outdoor dinner parties; other quilts are kept close at hand to ward off evening chills.

ABOVE: The small porch has a sweeping view. Here too, red and white come together to create a cozy atmosphere. Apple-shaped candles lined up along the porch railing add a touch of whimsy to the scene.

OPPOSITE: In the living room, two armless sofas covered in bold scarlet fabric are placed opposite each other; a third, more traditional design wears a red-and-white print that resembles a woven coverlet. The vaulted ceiling gives the combined living/dining area a sense of spaciousness. The farmhouse's original dark wood was left intact around the fireplace.

PAGE 72: More than forty fabric combinations were considered before the striped and floral seat covers were finally chosen. All of the dining room and living room chairs, pillows, and quilts match, making it easy to move them from one room to another and still keep the color theme consistent.

A CLOSER LOOK

COLOR
A dominant scheme of red and white unifies furniture, fabrics, and accessories in this farmhouse living room. Finding a common thread in items both large (the sofas) and small (the square picture frame) enlivens interiors.

COLLECTIONS
A pair of tin folk-art urns flanks a nineteenth-century French clock face. A stack of red-and-white quilts was positioned below one urn; beneath the other, a row of yellowware bowls displays bands of brownish-red.

PILLOWS
To balance the lively mixture of throw pillows, one design with a black background was placed on each sofa. The pillow in a floral print complements the country-style upholstery, and the elegant tapestry pillow looks just right on the scarlet sofa.

GROUNDING
When several patterns are used in a single setting, a few grounding elements can pull the look together. Here, sisal carpeting and black accents around the room, such as the coffee table, side tables, and clock face do the trick.

ABOVE: Tucked away on the second floor, this cozy bedroom's pure white walls have a gallery-like effect that is ideal for a series of black-and-white photographs in thick, black frames. The range of patterns—florals, checks, stars, and stripes—work perfectly together because they have the same color scheme and scale.

FARMHOUSE FAVORITE: PAINTED FLOORS

Looking for an unexpected spot to add a splash of color to a room? Consider the floor. Painted floors can provide a room's major source of color (sunny yellow in an all white bedroom, perhaps) or coordinate with the overall scheme (like the lavender-and-cream checkerboard in a purple bath on page 60). Painted floors were developed by Europeans in the snow country to bring lightness to floors and to beautify simple planks in imitation of costly parquet. Their popularity gives today's farmhouse decorators many patterns from which to choose for an authentic period look. Find wonderful patterns in magazines and books on decorative paint techniques. It's best to sand the floor before you begin, but if you are unable to prepare to that degree, thoroughly vacuum and mop the floor's surface to prevent dirt from mixing with the paint. Start with a primer coat (inquire at a local paint store about the best paint for your project) and finish with two to three coats of polyurethane to protect your work.

Chapter Three

FLEA MARKET STYLE

WHAT IS IT THAT DRAWS SO MANY OF US TO FLEA MARKETS, TAG SALES, AND YARD

SALES IN SEARCH OF UNIQUE FURNISHINGS AND UNUSUAL TREASURES? SOME PEOPLE

ENJOY THE THRILL OF THE HUNT, THE IDEA THAT THE PERFECT PIECE MAY TURN UP

AT ANY MOMENT. OTHERS APPRECIATE THE STORIES THAT SECONDHAND ITEMS

HAVE TO TELL ABOUT FORMER OWNERS AND DAYS GONE BY. ONE OF THE MOST

SPECIAL ASPECTS OF FLEA MARKET FINDS FROM AN INTERIOR DESIGN STANDPOINT

IS THEIR ABILITY TO CAPTURE A ONE-OF-A-KIND LOOK THAT PERSONALIZES A HOME

IN A WAY THAT MASS-PRODUCED FURNITURE SIMPLY CANNOT. FINALLY, THERE IS A

HEALTHY DOSE OF NOSTALGIA THAT GOES ALONG WITH DECORATING A HOME WITH

OLD THINGS—WHETHER THE OBJECTS HAIL FROM YOUR GREAT-GRANDMOTHER'S

LIFETIME OR YOUR OWN CHILDHOOD.

SWEET HOME

When a person has an affinity for the décor of a particular era, what better way to re-create the look at home than by using furnishings that were actually made during that period of time? For the owner of this 1850 farmhouse in Sullivan County, New York, the era in question is the period from the Great Depression to 1960. Her business—a bakery serving old-fashioned treats that could have been made in your grandmother's kitchen—reflects this love affair with the past; so does every room in her house. Flea market finds including early-twentieth-century furniture, lighting, artwork, appliances, table linens, and china lend authenticity to the interiors.

The home's decoration begins even before guests walk inside, on a wraparound porch furnished like an outdoor room with inviting rockers and an iron daybed dressed in vintage linens. Once indoors, the overall design scheme begins to charm the senses. Soft natural hues were chosen for the walls. Both wooden and upholstered furniture wear creamy coats of white, meaning that everything works in every room—a plus for the owner who gets the urge to rearrange things from time to time.

The spacious sage-green living room was once two smaller rooms; a dividing wall between the home's original parlor and second parlor was taken out to create the more fluid, open space. A wide archway leads from the living room to the dining room where warm ocher walls provide an easy transition for the eye.

While the living room and dining room each contain a healthy dose of vintage furnishings, it is the kitchen that looks most like a setting from the past. Just about everything in the butter-yellow room, from the chrome table to the dishtowels to the glass-front cabinets filled with period dishware and cookware, was discovered during flea-market forays. The vintage items are not simply decoration, however; they are all used as they were originally intended. Even the stove is from the 1950s and still works as well as ever. A coating of pale-gray paint on the floor sets a neutral stage for the flurry of color up above.

Butter-yellow paint was also used in the hallways and in the master bedroom, where the white chenille bedspread, white wicker nightstand, and lace curtains over the sunny bay window add restful touches. Little needed to be done to the master bath where the pedestal sink, medicine cabinet, and beaded-board paneling already exuded an old-fashioned feeling. Even the room's softly contrasting striped wallpaper—installed by a former owner—coordinated with the new décor's overall palette.

ABOVE: White slipcovers and throw pillows fashioned from vintage fabrics
dress the generously proportioned sofas. The slipcover in the living room has
a lovely pleated skirt. The whitewashed pie cupboard from the early 1900s
conceals evidence of the twenty-first century: a television and stereo system.
Directly opposite, another old cupboard houses books and collections. On
the floor, woven runners layered over sisal carpets add beauty and dimension
to the base of the room.

A CLOSER LOOK

APPLIANCES
Vintage appliances give a kitchen authentic retro style. Electrical repair shops can rewire almost anything. The six-burner Beautyrange by Odin, a "dream appliance" from the 1950s, had been sitting idle in a friend's garage before being installed here.

LINENS
Printed dishtowels, tablecloths, and aprons in cheerful floral patterns are some of the homeowner's favorite things to collect. Most are put to use; damaged textiles are recycled into curtains and pillow covers.

ARTWORK
Covers of old recipe pamphlets create a playful and colorful montage on the wall. Similar designs can be found at flea markets and thrift shops for a few dollars apiece. For a more formal look, the covers can be framed and hung in a row or grid pattern.

STOOL
A painted stool not only adds a splash of apple green to the room, it serves a practical purpose as well by supporting a vintage fan. Pulled up to the table, stove, or counter, it also acts as a useful surface during cooking and baking.

FLOORS
A pale shade of gray paint coats the floorboards, providing a pleasing contrast to the butter-yellow walls and an unexpected complement to the chrome stove and dining table. A braided rug occupies the area in front of the sink.

ABOVE: Mismatched wooden side chairs, unified by their white painted surfaces, surround a plank-top dining table. The antique oak bookcase with glass doors sees new service as storage for china and glassware and provides display space for a selection of McCoy pottery on top. A crystal chandelier and decorative tin wall sconces add a touch of glamour to the scene. Sheer curtains grace the windows.

FARMHOUSE FAVORITE: STORAGE

Farmhouses were not designed with modern storage needs in mind. Aside from the space-saving, built-in corner cabinets commonly seen in older structures, most farmhouses were constructed with very little storage space. Bedrooms, kitchens, and other living areas often lack closets, making additional storage units necessary. In the kitchen and dining areas many homeowners install large freestanding cupboards covered by glass doors to protect and display china, pottery, and other dinnerware. Sideboards are another popular choice for the dining room. They not only provide storage, they also act as an additional surface on which to set up displays or buffets for dinner parties. In the bedroom, armoires and dressers are common solutions for storing clothes and shoes, or they can be used to hide televisions, stereos, or other electronic equipment. Small trunks and blanket chests provide additional storage for pillows, throws, and quilts, while large baskets and hatboxes can hold small linens.

ABOVE AND OPPOSITE: The walls in the master bedroom are painted buttery yellow, which enhances the soft light. An old-fashioned chenille bedspread dresses the bed. The nightstand is also used as a display space for favorite finds such as a cut-glass lamp and vintage alarm clock, a graceful white McCoy vase, and a 1940s amateur still life of magnolias.

HUMBLE HOME

When we hear the word "hobby," it is most often an activity such as gardening or sewing that comes to mind. Not so for the owner of this Jeffersonville, New York, dwelling. His hobby is finding and restoring old farmhouses, and living in them until the next diamond-in-the-rough catches his eye. It is the simple architecture of the homes and the opportunity to breathe fresh life into long-neglected interiors that spurs his passion. His love of flea markets also serves him well in this pursuit; painted furniture, folk art, vintage kitchenware, table linens, trade signs, and architectural salvage are just a few of the treasures that give his home its signature look. His approach to renovation is the same with each house. First, structural concerns are addressed: the foundation, leaky roofs, drafty windows, and out-of-date wiring. Next, attention turns to interior design. A palette of crisp white for walls and sisal carpeting over refinished floorboards create a neutral background onto which furnishings and household accessories can be placed. Much of the furniture is painted white or covered in white slipcovers, making it easy to move items from room to room until the best mix is achieved.

The details of each individual room—a prominent mantel, perhaps, or a close proximity to the garden—influence the final appearance of each space. The living room of this gray-shingled farmhouse, for instance, lies just off the front porch. Garden antiques such as a weathered park bench, handmade birdhouse collection, and the whitewashed Adirondack love seat blur the line between indoors and out.

In the kitchen, new and old pieces work together to create a highly functional work space. The very practical modern island in the center of the room contrasts with the salvaged 1920s Magic Chef range, and mismatched knobs personalize the simple cabinetry. In the pantry, a green buffet, circa 1880, stands out against white horizontal beaded board. The breakfast nook's table and corner bench were discovered at a junk shop; a fresh coat of white paint gave the set new life.

A brass bed in the master bedroom was painted white and layered with a patchwork of brown-and-white sheets and blankets. Similar hues were used in the guest room, where a metal bed frame was refinished to give it the appearance of brushed chrome. An antique wooden trunk stands at the foot of the bed, easing the storage problem endemic to farmhouse bedrooms. The understated decoration is provided by engravings framed in gold, and an old dressmaker's form that assumes the look of a statue.

ABOVE: Sturdy items from the past find both a new home and
fresh uses in this parlor: The heavy planters of wrought iron make
excellent storage for magazines, and a classic kitchen table made
a good coffee table, once the legs were shortened. A tall green
cupboard keeps electronics out of sight when not in use. A burst
of color comes from a still life of blue objects on a side table.

ABOVE: Color can be the connection between collectibles, as opposed to shape or material. In this study in blue, the common color holds an array of disparate objects together, highlighting their shapes and textures. Small touches of green and white round out the serene display.

OPPOSITE: Hints of purple can be found throughout the dining room, from the gingham fabric on the chair seats to a large collection of purple-and-white table linens. (Mixing and matching tablecloths and napkins that vary in pattern but exhibit the same combination of colors creates a lively table setting.) On a sideboard, a collection of vintage white enamelware makes a strong visual statement. Lifted from a traditional setting, utilitarian objects can be appreciated for their shape and qualities. Few items in the collection are pristine, a fact that complements the casual feeling of the house and also makes it easier to find affordable additions to the group.

ABOVE: In the kitchen, furnishings are a blend of old and new as well: a very practical modern island table contrasts with a vintage Magic Chef range. Above the stove a vintage trade sign commands attention, and mismatched knobs on the cabinets add to the vintage feel of the room. A hanging two-tier dish rack keeps big and small plates close at hand above the double sink. Overhead, a curvaceous chandelier adds an elegant touch.

OPPOSITE: The owner's collection of sepia architectural photographs and aging pen-and-ink drawings inspired the master bedroom's restful palette of soft browns. The brass bed was painted white and layered with an array of light-brown linens.

ABOVE: In the guest bedroom, paint was stripped from the metal bed to give it the appearance of brushed chrome. A wooden trunk provides additional storage. Blankets, bed linens, and bedspreads can be mixed and matched endlessly to create a fresh look.

When house hunting, some people have a precise image in their head of what their new home should look like. The owners of this charming farmhouse were searching for "a house in a field, alone at the end of a quiet country road." They found exactly that on an old dairy farm in Sullivan County, New York. There was only one problem: the early-1900s dwelling was in a terrible state of disrepair. Undaunted, the couple purchased the house and began a respectful restoration that updated the interior for contemporary living while maintaining the austerity of the original architecture. A palette of white for walls and furniture under-scores the home's simple décor; creative groupings of flea-market finds add a touch of twenty-first-century style.

On the first floor, six interior walls were removed to create an open floor plan. At the center of the layout is a staircase leading upstairs. The living area lies to one side of the steps, the dining room to the other. A large custom-built cupboard abuts the living-room side of the staircase. The oak floorboards wear a dark stain similar in shade to the exposed beams overhead and the main countertop of the large cupboard.

In the dining area, a set of six wooden side chairs with wonderfully chipping paint sur-rounds a long barn-wood table. Beaded-board wainscoting gives the walls an old-fashioned feeling and differentiates the space from the living area. French doors leading to the porch were installed on one end of the room to facilitate outdoor dining in mild weather.

A spacious country kitchen was high on the list of must-haves for the house. Details throughout the sunny space impart an old-fashioned look, and new overhead cupboards were built to replicate the original cupboards near the sink. A classic country cupboard with glass doors up top and paneled doors below was constructed of wood salvaged from old Vermont barns. On the shelves, the owners' affinity for subtle hints of blue—this time in the form of vintage ceramics, glass, and enamelware—is apparent.

Upstairs, cozy bedrooms share the same comfortable simplicity as the rest of the house. In the guest room, beaded-board wainscoting reaches eye level, while a warm butter yellow coats the upper walls. A gracefully curved iron bed is dressed with white sheets and a quilted floral bedcover. Artwork and decorative details are kept to a minimum in all the bedrooms, resulting in thoroughly restful spaces.

ABOVE: A custom-built cabinet offers ample storage for everyday china on its upper shelves and toys in the cabinets below. A mixture of plush white seating and whitewashed pieces with well-worn surfaces (including a trunk serving as a coffee table and a low cupboard beside an armchair) energizes the living room. Accents of blue and blue-green can be seen around the room—a ceramic bowl, an old toolbox, a manual typewriter, and so on. Even the staircase displays a touch of blue along the front panel of each step.

OPPOSITE: In the large, sun-filled kitchen, beaded-board cabinet doors and a butcher-block top enhance the new island; the useful piece rests on wheels so it can be rolled aside or to a new location. In keeping with their thoughtful restoration, the refrigerator and stove are restored vintage models, the stove having been discovered at an online auction. The "Milk" sign above the stove was once attached to the property's barn.

OPPOSITE: The kitchen cabinet was built in Vermont from reclaimed barn wood. The blue-and-white dish-ware has origins elsewhere: South Africa, Tennessee, and New York State.

RIGHT (top): The homeowners wanted to honor the history of the old farmhouse. One of their first acquisitions, a vintage poster depicting a mother cow and her calf that hangs above the table, is a nod to the property's previous incarnation as a dairy farm.

RIGHT (bottom): In the guest bedroom, a tabletop arrangement combines an alabaster lamp, a white ironstone ewer, a pressed-glass bowl filled with pinecones, and a Depression glass cake stand now functioning as a candleholder.

FARMHOUSE FAVORITE: OLD MIRRORS

A frequent sight at flea markets across the country, antique and vintage mirrors can impart instant farmhouse style in any room. They can be hung in a traditional manner—in a foyer or above a bathroom sink, for example, or employed in unexpected ways, such as a single mirror positioned above a tabletop still life or a collection of mirrors displayed on an empty wall. Although many people appreciate the look of worn silver in an antique mirror, anyone wishing to find replacement mirror glass for their mirror can inquire at a glass store. Frames, too, can be altered to suit your taste or to suit a particular setting, whether you choose to strip them or repaint them. For old-fashioned flair, let well-worn frames remain as you found them.

ABOVE: Bead-board wainscoting was added to the guest bedroom to give the room a country feel. The only ornament on the wall: a simple mirror positioned above the bed.

PICTURE PERFECT

"Good bones" are what all people on the market for an old house are looking for. A house may appear uninhabitable, but if the structure is basically sound and the interior exhibits pleasing proportions and original details, some adventurous soul (or souls) will gladly accept the challenge to restore the dwelling to its former grandeur. The 1859 Granville, Ohio, farmhouse pictured on these pages was "dilapidated" when its current owners spotted it late in the 1990s. A nearby barn (shown at left) stood on the verge of collapse. Plumbing and wiring had been updated in the house, but very little else had been maintained to any degree over the years. Still, the husband and wife could see those "good bones" and the setting couldn't be beat. Rolling hills, verdant fields, and a quiet pond comprised the view.

The renovation had three stages, or themes: clean, color, and collections. First, the interior was stripped of old paint and wallpaper. A fresh coat of white paint on the ceiling drew attention to the home's exposed beams on the first floor. Sanding and a new stain rejuvenated the oak floorboards throughout. When the rooms were once again hospitable, soft colors were painted on the walls—pale apple green in the dining room, butterscotch in the kitchen, a whisper of aqua in the master bedroom. As a finishing touch, comfortable furniture and cherished objects gathered at flea markets and antiques shops were arranged in each room, creating interiors that epitomize contemporary farmhouse style.

Some of the most personal touches in the home are the husband's paintings. In the dining room, the wall space above the sideboard has been designated as a showcase for large landscapes that are rotated with the seasons—an autumn view in the fall, a snowy scene in the winter, and so on. The creative eye of his wife, a milliner by trade, can be seen in the house in the artfully arranged still lifes that incorporate fruit, foliage, and collections.

In contrast to the rich colors and strong lines found on the first floor of the house, the mood in the master bedroom is light and serene. Aqua paint on the walls is complemented by possessions of pale green. A new floral quilted bedcover from Provence dresses the whitewashed iron bed, and a sheer white curtain flutters at the window.

OPPOSITE: A loving, and timely, rehabilitation rescued the barn from near-collapse (see the exterior on page 102). Now the soaring interior serves as a painting studio. Finished works cover the back wall of the barn, and the seating area in front of the wall is furnished with a brown leather armchair and sofa to comfortably entertain clients. A commanding mirror reflects sunlight and visually expands the space. Even in this casual setting, attractive still lifes raise everyday objects to artistic heights. The artist's paintbrushes fill blown-glass vases (this page, right).

ABOVE: The kitchen itself is like a work of art: Molding and beaded board were installed during the renovation to add architectural detail to the room. A graphic black-and-white checkerboard pattern makes the floor an integral part of the overall décor. A stack of antique books rests atop a mustard-yellow side table; a weathered garden urn discovered at Ohio's famed Springfield Antique Show Extravaganza (a biannual event held in May and September) sits on the table's bottom shelf.

OPPOSITE: A fall landscape painting by the artist complements the seasonal still-life atop the sideboard. The homeowners change the painting each season.

ABOVE: Portraits of the couple's son and daughter hang on either side of a blue-painted jelly cupboard from the late 1800s, also in the dining room. The jelly cupboard is used to store pottery and glassware.

ABOVE: In the master bedroom, a distinct collecting sensibility is apparent. A painted mirror on the wall, a garden bench at the foot of the bed, and a cluster of McCoy and Roseville pottery atop a towering cupboard wearing exquisitely aged, pale-green paint. Next to the cupboard, the mate to the kitchen's white garden urn holds delicate privet berries.

A CLOSER LOOK

COLOR

Blue-painted furniture can be found in a wide range of shades that complement each other when positioned side by side, as this desk and dresser illustrate. This bedroom's aqua walls and soft green floors further emphasize the decorative possibilities of a monochromatic palette.

DESK

Topped with an antique letter sorter, an old farm table functions as a writing desk. Many types of tables found at flea markets can be similarly employed. The best style for your home depends on the amount of work space you need and the dimensions of the room.

COLLECTIONS

White McCoy vases, antique books, and silhouettes number among the owners' favorite things. Included in the silhouette collection are depictions of the couple's two children. Installing a narrow art shelf creates extra display space in cozy settings such as this.

CHAIR

As with tables, there are many styles of chair to be found at flea markets, second-hand stores and tag sales that can be used as desk chairs. Rolling designs like this whitewashed example are especially practical. Well-worn chairs can be repainted or stripped, and torn seats replaced with cheerful fabric.

Chapter Four

COLLECTIONS

When visiting the home of a collector, one is almost sure to find

pleasant surprises at every turn. While many of us view tabletops as

fine places for plates, and bookshelves as suitable storage for books,

collectors consider every surface and niche as potential display space.

As a result, each room becomes a gallery for precious possessions. A

dining-room sideboard might support an arrangement of dinnerware or

unexpected items like cast-iron toy trucks. Kitchen windowsills might

be lined with light-catching glass, while a bathroom sink could act as

a stage for vintage perfume bottles. Even a staircase can be utilized—

with one vintage sprinkler or stoneware crock placed on the side of

each step. For more creative ideas, peruse the following pages.

ABOVE: Walls of pale wheat and black-painted floors
set a graphic yet understated tone in the dining room
where four unpainted wicker armchairs surround a
one-of-a-kind table. To make the table, a salvaged
portion of column was used for the base and a circular
piece of beveled glass became the top.

A PASSION FOR COLLECTING

It is the rare dealer in antiques whose home is not a showcase for collections. This Upstate New York farmhouse, whose owners run a local antiques shop, is a prime example of this truism. Each room—from the most public to the most private—harbors artfully arranged treasures. Some of the collections are traditional (yellowware bowls, mercury glass, and alabaster) while others are somewhat quirky (bocce balls, finials, and wind-up alarm clocks). No matter how historically significant or wonderfully whimsical an object might be, each is given equal decorative weight in this household.

In the living room, the owners' unique collecting vision becomes apparent. Limestone spheres queue up on one edge of the mantel, bocce balls are piled in a bowl on a side table, and diminutive lidded pots are clustered on the coffee table. The pairing of unconventional objects with staid surroundings is part of the fun of decorating with collections.

The dining room features stately cabinets with roomy glass-front cupboards on top to house collections. One side is filled with nineteenth-century mercury glass, made by sandwiching a silvery substance between identical glass molds. A variety of objects fills the other side of the cupboard, including gracefully carved alabaster candlesticks, jars, and compotes. Care was taken during the placement of these pieces to balance tall and short pieces, thin and wide, ornate and simple.

As fitting as a display of mixing bowls in a kitchen, the owners' collection of vintage wind-up alarm clocks looks right at home on a bedside table in the guest room. On a well-weathered table nearby, a selection of salvaged finials (originally destined for curtain poles) pairs well with the wallpaper's dramatic urn motif.

Putting a collection of French doors to good use in the bath, the owners constructed a screen that shelters a clawfoot tub. A 1920s marble sink, resting on the legs of salvaged cast-iron gutter pipe, supports another collection in the room: porcelain pots manufactured in England to hold such products as anchovy paste, toothpaste, dry mustard, ointments, and salves. The tiny lidded jars (most measure about two inches in diameter) are lined up in two neat rows.

A CLOSER LOOK

MANTEL
A natural focal point in a room, the mantel is often the site of eye-catching collections. To create this asymmetrical display, a central work of art is flanked by a mantel clock on one side and a quartet of limestone spheres on the other.

COFFEE TABLE
Large coffee tables are ideal spots for collections of all kinds. Here, small lidded pots are clustered in the center of the table, leaving ample space all around for family and friends to rest a magazine or a cup of tea.

SIDE TABLES
Positioned beside the sofa and between the armchairs, two side tables support artful arrangements. Each display features a tall element surrounded by several smaller pieces. The placement of footed bowls on each table draws the eye from one display to the other.

BOOKS
Books can function as attractive accessories in a room. Here, volumes are stacked on a leather-upholstered stool and a side table next to the sofa. Topping the stacks with a small, cherished object underscores their decorative placement.

ABOVE: In the bathroom, a screen was created out of old French doors purchased at auction. The 1920s sink rests on legs constructed out of salvaged cast-iron gutter pipe. A wrought-iron garden chair is positioned below the window to hold towels. Single side chairs are another favorite collection of the homeowners, who use them elsewhere in the house in a similar fashion—to add visual interest while stylishly holding towels, magazines, potted plants, and more.

PAGE 117: Mirrored Art Deco bed frames enhance the guest bedroom's elegant look. Overhead, charcoal-gray paint similar in hue to the urns on the wallpaper draws attention to the ceiling's intricate woodwork. A collection of wind-up clocks gives the room a quirky charm.

FARMHOUSE FAVORITE: QUILT RACKS

Quilt racks are a sensible and stylish means of display, not only for quilts but also for all manner of textiles, such as woven coverlets, Beacon blankets, and lace-edged linens. Filled with vibrant or intricately patterned pieces, a quilt rack's placement within the home can add a burst of color or a touch of texture to any room. In addition to their decorative qualities, textile collections displayed on a quilt rack can also serve a practical purpose. Consider printed tablecloths or dishtowels in a kitchen, embroidered hand towels in a powder room, or crocheted afghans beside a cozy reading chair. Old quilt racks occasionally surface at antiques stores and flea markets; for new designs, inquire at a local quilt shop.

GEORGIA GEM

Can a passion for collecting help a person find his or her dream house? It did for the owner of this farmhouse in Roswell, Georgia. The charming residence sits along the route to its current owner's favorite flea market. Each time he drove past, he would gaze longingly at the home. One day he noticed a "For Sale" sign outside, and the rest is history. Built in 1901, the farmhouse had been well kept over the years. Fresh coats of paint were all that was necessary to ready the interior for a copious collection of country antiques and colorful accessories. Pale-wheat and butter-yellow paint on the upper portions of the walls and pure white on the beaded board below create a unified backdrop throughout much of the house.

A photographer by trade, the owner arranged pretty vignettes throughout the house, aided by the objects' similar styling, warm tones, and weathered surfaces. The visual treat begins on the front porch, where a painted garden bench hosts an ever-changing still life of interesting objects—old watering cans, weathered shutters, and architectural elements, to name a few. Once inside, the show continues. Family photographs in a wide variety of old frames line the wainscoting in the entrance hall.

The colors of the collections set the tone in certain rooms. Pieces chosen for the study, for instance, are somewhat subdued in hue—a late-1800s drafting table, a whitewashed gate, and a curvy wooden armchair with a black leather seat. The most intense color in the room comes from the red, white, and blue barber pole. By contrast, lighthearted pastels made their way into the dining room, where lively dinner parties are often held. Seltzer bottles of colored glass stand guard along the dining room mantel, while hand-painted Blue Ridge pottery from the 1930s and 1940s fills a blue-painted Hoosier cabinet with its original flour sifter still intact.

Bright white paint refreshed the kitchen's walls, cabinetry, and beaded-board ceiling. Collections in this quaint setting are traditionally associated with a kitchen, including enamelware, wooden milk buckets, and a hanging grocery scale. The items that furnish the bathroom, on the other hand, are transplants from other rooms: an antique butter churn, a wooden step stool, a vintage fan, an oil lamp, and an old-time radio.

ABOVE: The drafting table in the study was one of
the homeowner's first acquisitions. Objects with
well-worn surfaces are a favorite; here, the weathered
surfaces and muted colors of his flea-market finds
imbue the room with character and charm.

ABOVE (left): The dining room features an early-1900s Hoosier cabinet.
On top of the cabinet, two vintage kitchen scales and an amateur portrait
discovered in a thrift shop make a simple, pleasing display.

ABOVE (right): A powder blue Murano-glass chandelier hangs above the
dining table. Mismatched side chairs surround the table; the range of colors
and styles is in keeping with the mood of the room.

OPPOSITE: On the kitchen's wood floor, the owner painted a checkerboard pattern in black and white—the only addition made to this room. A hanging grocery scale and a collection of milk buckets lend an old-fashioned feeling.

ABOVE: Removing objects from their traditional settings—such as the radio and the butter churn—focuses attention on their unique forms. The exterior of the claw-foot tub had been painted blue by a previous owner; rather than repaint it, the current owner chose towels and a woven rug to match. The mirrors on the wall behind the tub date to the early 1900s.

In some collectors' homes, different objects are displayed in different rooms—Depression glass in the kitchen, for example, and quilts in the bedroom. A single, sizable collection of nineteenth-century china populates all the public rooms in this farmhouse in Bucks County, Pennsylvania, constructed around 1800. Blue-and-white transferware brightens the living room, pink lusterware inspired the palette in the sitting room, mulberry ware (transferware with a deep purple hue) makes a dramatic statement in the dining room, and white iron-stone complements the country kitchen's casual atmosphere. Before one box of plates could be unpacked, however, the house itself needed quite a bit of work. A new roof, new plumbing, and new wiring were all imperative. Among the qualities that attracted the owner despite the extensive renovations were the original woodwork throughout and numerous bookcases and built-in cupboards—ideal for her collections.

Butter-yellow walls and furniture sheathed in pale floral damasks create an oasis of calm and comfort in the living room. The golden hues also pair well with the blue-and-white transferware housed in a fireside cupboard. To increase the cupboard's storage capacity, small hooks were screwed into the bottom of one shelf so that teacups could be hung there. To reveal a bit of the dwelling's history, the peeling plaster on the cupboard's interior was left untouched.

Although the shelves built into the sitting room were originally intended for books, the owner saw immediately that they would serve as the perfect display space for her large collection of pink lusterware. Spillover from the bookshelves was thoughtfully arranged on the mantel. The pale, khaki paint that coats the walls was chosen in part because it went well with the pink-and-white china. The toile, seersucker, and cottage rose upholstery fabrics echo the color scheme of the lusterware.

Heeding a friend's advice that "life is too short to live with neutrals," the owner painted the dining room walls metallic gold. In addition to its overall energizing effect, the wall color makes the mulberry ware in the built-in cupboard really stand out in the space. As in the sitting room, black accents are spread throughout: the decoratively painted dining chairs, gingham-upholstered armchair, lampshade, and picture frame.

ABOVE: On the living room mantel, one gold-rimmed teacup and saucer set, known as wedding-band china, sits on each end; the gilded edge is mirrored in the decorative lamp bases, a gold frame, and gold ornaments on the front of the mantel. The primitive portrait over the mantel is a print of a mid-1800s original; a gold frame gives it an air of importance and, from a distance, the appearance of a period painting.

RIGHT: Black accents such as an applied mantel ornament, a Vermont granite slab on the radiator, and a lampshade on an alabaster lamp punctuate the sunny sitting room. Hooked rugs in floral motifs from the late 1800s cover the floors.

ABOVE: The dining room's walls are painted metallic gold, which complements the collection of transferware displayed in the built-in cupboard. The elegant crystal-beaded chandelier adds a touch of sparkle overhead. A trio of antique pitchers rests on the deep windowsill.

FARMHOUSE FAVORITE: WHITE IRONSTONE

During its heyday in the mid-1800s, white ironstone china was so popular in rural areas that it became known as farmer's china. Small wonder, then, that its use in contemporary interiors instills instant farmhouse charm. Homemakers of the past appreciated the ware's durability and simple, sculptural forms. Today's collectors feel much the same way. One difference between then and now, however, is that where a farm family would likely settle on one pattern for their dinner service and serving pieces, collectors often accumulate as many patterns as they can find. Display ideas include filling a cupboard with a variety of shapes, sizes, and styles, lining pitchers along a high shelf, or hanging platters against a colorful wall.

ABOVE: Pale yellow coats walls and cabinetry in the kitchen. A salvaged six-foot-long porcelain sink looks as if it were made to fit beneath the room's windows. Ironstone pitchers parade along the windowsill, while plates, bowls, and a tureen or two are kept on a high shelf overhead. Displaying the collection on open shelves not only draws attention to variations in size and pattern, it also keeps the pieces close at hand for everyday use. Marble countertops and pressed-glass cabinet knobs and drawer pulls are new additions that emphasize the room's old-fashioned style.

A CASUAL LOOK

Some houses silently accept the possessions of each new inhabitant; others seem to dictate what decorative style will work best. The latter is true of this 1838 stone farmhouse in Pennsylvania's Brandywine Valley. This was a casual house that needed a casual look. For this reason, some of the more formal furnishings and accessories from the owner's previous residence did not make the trip, including a collection of Staffordshire figurines. Instead, country antiques and respectful reproductions were chosen to give the interior an early-nineteenth-century air.

Though the interior was in good shape overall, some renovation was necessary in certain rooms. For example, the pine-paneled living room, located in a 1950s addition, had a distinctly mid-twentieth-century feel to it. Once the paneling was removed, the stone fireplace was stuccoed over and a circa 1840 mantel was installed in its place. An ordinary door was replaced with an early-1800s grain-painted example.

Pastoral views through the dining room's nine-over-nine windows inspired the setting's pale, earthy palette. Reproduction seating surrounds the French table of 1830 with a tilt top and shoe feet. Homespun feed sacks stenciled with the names of local farmers were fashioned into down-filled seat cushions for the rush-seat armchairs, evidence of the owner's interest in inventing new uses for everyday items from the past. In the kitchen, the six-over-six window is topped by a coordinating valance that was crafted from a linen tea towel. Diminutive antiques—including a family of figural cookie cutters and a cluster of Shaker-style boxes—are arranged on a hanging shelf.

In the master bedroom, the owner gathered a few favorite things from her collections to place beside her bed. On one nightstand, a mercury glass vase tops a stack of books; the books act as both pedestal and reading material. A tower of early-nineteenth-century band-boxes rests on the other nightstand. Nearby, a glass-front cupboard houses some of the owner's most precious possessions: lengths of antique fabric, including red, indigo, and butterscotch homespun grouped by color. Vintage ribbon, decorative pin cushions, and painted pantry boxes share shelf space with the treasured textiles.

ABOVE: Collections in the pared-down living room are used sparingly. A graduated set of handled baskets tops a cupboard, while above the mantel a late-1800s hooked rug is flanked by painted tin sconces. Neat stacks of books on the coffee table take on the appearance of another collection.

LEFT: Open shelves beside the doorway are lined with a large collection of rare, salt-glazed, stoneware crocks with cobalt figures; the most visually intriguing of the group are placed at eye level. Yellowware pitchers and bowls populate the top shelf.

BELOW: In the kitchen, pale-yellow paint on the floor complements a pair of mid-1800s plank-seat side chairs as well as the owner's collection of yellowware. Grouping small items together prevents them from becoming lost in more expansive settings. A vibrant early-1900s rug adds a splash of color to the scene.

A CLOSER LOOK

WORK SPACE
The office is located in the original 1838 portion of the house. For the owner, an interior designer, a large work surface was a must. In place of a traditional desk, she chose a four-drawer Pennsylvania worktable from the 1860s.

COLLECTIONS
Displaying cherished objects in a home office can spark creative ideas. Antique textiles are a passion for this home-owner; homespun feed sacks with the names of local farmers stenciled onto them are pinned up around the room.

STORAGE
A large basket beside the desk keeps fabric swatches, throw pillows, and other remnants close at hand while projects are ongoing. When needed, a long bench across the room can support file folders, stacks of quilts, and reference books.

LADDER
Like the bench, the 1870s English ladder resting in the corner can be put to use when additional space is called for. Among the items that can be draped over the rungs are fabrics and home design magazines opened to inspiring pages.

OPPOSITE: French quilts from the middle of the nineteenth century and a hand-painted silk pillow dress a reproduction tester bed of tiger-maple. The romantic dust ruffle and bed hanging were made from cream-colored silk taffeta. The blue-and-cream boxes inspired the overall color scheme of the room.

Chapter Five

ANTIQUES

ANTIQUES AND FARMHOUSES ARE A NATURAL PAIR. BOTH CONNECT US WITH OUR

ROOTS. BUT DECORATING WITH ANTIQUES DOES NOT MEAN THAT EVERY PIECE MUST

MATCH THE DATE OF THE HOUSE—THERE ARE MANY WAYS TO INTERPRET THE LOOK.

THE HOUSES FEATURED IN THIS CHAPTER SHOW A GOOD CROSS SECTION OF HOW

ANTIQUES ARE USED TODAY. IN ONE INSTANCE, EARLY AMERICAN ANTIQUES

RE-CREATE THE TYPICAL INTERIORS FROM THE TIME WHEN THE FARMHOUSE WAS

CONSTRUCTED. ANOTHER HOME MARRIES PERIOD FURNITURE WITH FINE REPRODUC-

TIONS MADE BY THE OWNER HIMSELF. A THIRD EXAMPLE SETS ELEGANT PIECES

AGAINST A THOROUGHLY MODERN COLOR SCHEME OF PALE PUMPKIN, CELERY,

AND BUTTER YELLOW, WHILE A FOURTH COMBINES ANTIQUE, VINTAGE, AND NEW

FURNISHINGS IN A COMFORTABLE MIX THAT IS "GRANDCHILD FRIENDLY."

ABOVE: In the kitchen, a painted cupboard displays collections of cobalt-decorated stoneware, blue-and-white coverlets, and late-nineteenth-century American baskets. Banister-back chairs pull up to a hutch table crafted in Maine in the 1840s. Pewter pieces placed above the mantel remind one of the home's early American origins.

ONE LAYER AT A TIME

For one Connecticut couple, restoring an early-nineteenth-century farmhouse was truly a labor of love. Though previous owners had been respectful of the dwelling, much work was needed to revive its historical integrity. Asbestos siding was stripped from the exterior. Indoors, rotting beams were replaced, cracked floorboards pulled up, and walls were replastered. Then, wallpaper in patterns of the period, painted finishes, and stenciled floor patterns were put in place. When the project was complete, a large collection of Early American antiques—many with colorful painted finishes—was positioned throughout the house, creating rooms that look just as they might have when the house was built two centuries ago.

Splashes of red (one owner's favorite color) appear in many rooms, including the living room. Cranberry-colored curtains are draped dramatically at the windows, while a scarlet wing chair sits beside a green sofa dotted with red-and-white textiles. Woodwork in the room is painted to match the background of the printed wallpaper, creating a cohesive and cozy look. On the floor, a painted lattice and fleur-de-lis pattern adds visual interest.

Years before the current owners bought the house, the dining room floor had been sanded too rigorously, leaving the oak floorboards stained and uneven. To remedy the situation, the owners enlisted a decorative artist to camouflage the damage by painting a marblized black-and-white checkerboard pattern. For the wall, a complex paint treatment using rags, sandpaper, and glaze gave the muted pink color an aged appearance. Silhouettes in original frames are displayed around the room, bringing an authentic air to walls as well as surfaces.

Red woodwork distinguishes the family sitting room, once known as the keeping room on farms far from the Eastern Seaboard. The room's original wide-plank oak floor was hidden beneath three layers of wood flooring. Salvaged floorboards from a local house of the same period were used to replace the areas that had been eaten away by carpenter ants. So devoted were the owners to historical accuracy, they even found period bricks to replace deteriorating ones inside the hearth.

Bedrooms are as period perfect as the other rooms in the house, and each has its own personality. The guest room has casual country charm, and gray painted floorboards and red woodwork set against cream-colored walls underscore the simplicity of the scene. The master bedroom received a more formal treatment, re-creating a bedchamber that would have been found in an affluent home of the day.

ABOVE: Painted floors and stenciled walls are among the formal dining room's classic nineteenth-century details. Chairs of curly maple with can seats surround a mahogany Hepplewhite dining table. The owners' found the unusual curtain fabric in an antiques shop in Newport, Rhode Island; it combines pink toile with images of sixteenth- and seventeenth-century historical figures.

OPPOSITE: The owner collaborated with local artisans to paint the home's floors. Here, a fleur-de-lis pattern graces the living room's hardwood floor. A stately grandfather clock and early-1800s mirror hung between the windows are elegant touches.

A CLOSER LOOK

DÉCOR
Period furniture and accessories re-create a bedroom as it might have looked in the early 1800s, around the time the house was built. The elegant canopy bed, Hepplewhite shield-back side chairs, and four-drawer dresser are all typical of wealthy homes of the Federal era.

COLOR
Traces of red—the owner's favorite color—appear in many rooms in the house. In the master bedroom it comes in the form of red-and-cream toile. The owner came across ten yards of the fabric in an antiques shop and used every inch of it to make window treatments, slipcovers, and a bed skirt.

FLOOR
A decorative artist was hired to stencil a floral-and-latticework pattern on the floor. The design is based on a historical example the owner admired during a visit to Colonial Williamsburg, in Williamsburg, Virginia. Several coats of polyurethane protect the lively pattern.

ARTWORK
Decoration on the walls includes both traditional ornaments (such as the portrait of a young man and the ebony-and-gold mirror in the corner by the bed) and untraditional choices (the lacquered tray above the vanity mirror). The tray adds another dash of red to the scene.

ABOVE: An artful mix of antiques and colors give the house a warm, comfortable atmosphere. Arranged with an artistic eye, a stack of buckets and two pitchers make an attractive composition.

LEFT: On the wall in the guest bedroom, a silk crib quilt hangs above a collection of nineteenth-century doll clothes suspended on a small rack. Ample space is left between the tiny dresses so that the humble artistry of each can be appreciated. A graphic quilt dating to the late 1800s adorns the bed.

When it came time to decorate their 1860 farmhouse in Southampton, New York, one couple had two directives: the interior should reflect their passion for collecting antiques while remaining "grandchild friendly." To achieve this uncommon combination, centuries-old furniture and accessories were placed alongside vintage pieces and new designs. Everything, no matter its age or origin, can be sat upon, opened up, or used. Comfort is key.

In the sunny living room, upholstered pieces are new while wooden chests, benches, and desks are old. A number of the antiques have been assigned new uses, such as the spool-legged table with drop leaves that is now used as a desk and a painted garden bench transformed into a useful table next to a sofa. The settee in the window bay was constructed by reconfiguring an Early American cherry bed. Original to the house, an arched corner cupboard safeguards a collection of McCoy vases. French doors lead from the living room to the dining room, where a collapsible nineteenth-century French wine tasting table can fit a party of sixteen. Other antiques in the room include a pie safe-turned-linen cupboard and framed prints on the wall.

The kitchen's farm table was hidden by an oilcloth when the owners found it. Stripped and refinished, the table now acts as command central, where the couple plans their daily schedule. A painted garden bench on one side of the table accommodates multiple grandchildren at one sitting. Roomy cupboards are a favorite find of the owners, who prefer freestanding furniture in place of built-in cabinets.

The master bedroom is a serene getaway, awash in soft greens and yellows. The inviting collection of linens that dress the antique iron bed are a mix of old and new; a green-and-white quilt from the late 1800s lies beneath a plush striped duvet and throw pillows covered in vintage chintz. Among the room's whimsical touches are baby chick garden ornaments and salvaged stained glass windows above the fireplace, and a vintage model boat across the room on a nineteenth-century chest of drawers. Left bare, the oak floorboards reflect the stripes of the wallpaper up above.

OPPOSITE: In the dining room, a pie safe is used as a linen cupboard. The table is a collapsible French wine-tasting table that seats sixteen. The arched corner cabinet is original to the house and holds a collection of matte-white McCoy pottery. The pale yellow chosen for the walls offers a pleasing continuity with the soft yellows of the living room.

ABOVE: Soft colors and architectural details provide a classic backdrop to the comfortable yet sophisticated living room. The ledge of the living room's period paneling serves as an easel for favorite framed prints and a gilded triptych mirror from the late 1800s. The windows were intentionally left bare in order to maximize natural light. A goose decoy surveys the scene from its perch atop a nineteenth-century cupboard, while a drop-leaf spool-legged table now serves as a desk.

OPPOSITE: The farm table was covered in oilcloth when the owner's found it. Refinished, it now holds sway in the kitchen. The green cupboard, made from old barn wood, functions as a pantry; a collection of ceramic pitchers is stored on top. The tall case-clock is a family heirloom; it was a gift to the homeowner's grandfather commemorating a lifetime of service as a stationmaster for the Pennsylvania Railroad.

ABOVE: The master bedroom is a serene retreat of luxurious linens and plenty of natural light. A fluffy down comforter and a mix of old and new linens dress the bed. The botanical print above the bed is matted in green and framed in gold, picking up the two dominant colors in the space.

FARMHOUSE FAVORITE: CLAW-FOOT TUBS

Few bathroom fixtures capture farmhouse style as well as the claw-foot bathtub. These old-fashioned designs can stand alone as a tub or be fitted with a showerhead and circular shower curtain. Antique examples surface in salvage shops and used furniture stores; new models are made by a number of companies and are available through bathroom showrooms and restoration catalogs. Old tubs have a sense of history that many homeowners appreciate, but keep in mind that the porcelain on antique pieces may need resurfacing and the hardware replaced. And don't forget that claw-foot originals are extremely heavy. This is a major consideration if you need to install it in a second- or third-floor bathroom. Although the most classic look for the claw-foot tub is pure white, inside and out, some creative homeowners paint the tub's exterior to coordinate with the color scheme of the room.

ABOVE: Part of a guest room was transformed into a luxurious master bath. Beaded-board paneling imparts an old-fashioned feeling, while the oversized, cream-and-yellow checkerboard floor pattern is a fresh twist on a traditional decorative paint technique. The vanity was custom-made to match the beaded board and fitted with a drop-in sink surrounded by marble. The six-foot-long claw-foot tub is a wonderful place to dream; it can also fit six toddlers at a time, speeding up the bath routine when all eleven grandchildren are in residence.

RESTORING MEMORIES

When their weekend home, an 1810 farmhouse filled with heirlooms and antiques, burned to the ground, this couple refused to be defeated by their loss. Instead, they turned misfortune into an opportunity to improve on a house and a lifestyle they had grown to love. From a collection of photographs, an architect and a builder were able to replicate the Federal-period farmhouse. Details such as plaster walls, restoration glass windows, raised panel doors, and salvaged wide-plank pine floorboards gave the structure the look of an old house. To bring the same sense of history to the interiors, the owners visited their favorite antiques shops in the nearby town of Hudson, New York, and attended local auctions to find gems from the eighteenth and nineteenth centuries. Because the farmhouse is often a gathering place for family and friends, the antiques needed to be practical, with surfaces that would only be enhanced by wear.

For the living room, the couple chose to update the color scheme they'd had before. Pale green paint coats woodwork while the pumpkin color chosen for the walls is a few shades lighter than the one in their former residence. The crown molding above the windows is painted gold, echoing the hue of an antique mirror as well as the gilded frames enclosing old prints and paintings around the room. A Victorian painting depicting an imperiled mother dog and her pups claims a place of honor above a new mantel modeled after an antique design. Wooden side chairs from the nineteenth century provide additional seating as well as decorative focal points throughout the room.

Pale pumpkin and green paint also cast their soothing spell over the dining room. The early-1800s black walnut farm table was chosen for its length as well as its resemblance to the table that had been lost in the fire. Furnishings with old green painted finishes are a particular favorite of the couple. Evidence of this preference can be seen throughout the house, especially in the kitchen where the breakfast area is populated by an attractive grouping of side chairs, a dining table, and a sculptural stepladder. Another study in green can be found in the family room, where a salvaged mid-1800s mantel features green and mustard paint. Around this central element, green objects have been lovingly placed.

OPPOSITE: The homeowners searched for furnishings with interesting silhouettes, like this country rocking chair with a tombstone-shaped back. Their affinity for green is reflected in the glass candlesticks, sap buckets, and an antique portrait of a young woman wearing a green dress. Even the leaves in the hooked rug on the floor exhibit the beloved faded green hue.

ABOVE: The color scheme in the living room is an updated version of the one they'd had before—pale gray-green on the woodwork, pumpkin on the walls, and gold crown molding above the windows.

A CLOSER LOOK

COLOR
Pale pumpkin and soft green are a favorite color combination of the residents. Here, walls are painted with a whisper of pumpkin, while woodwork wears green. The ceiling is an even lighter version of the trim, to avoid one of the owner's pet peeves: large expanses of white.

SEATING
Because their dining room is often the hub of get-togethers of family and friends, the couple amassed a large collection of nineteenth-century Hitchcock side chairs. When more people must be squeezed around the table, a garden bench beneath the sideboard is called upon.

SIDEBOARD
A long worktable makes a handsome sideboard. The base retains its original green paint—a fact that first attracted the owners, who love antique furniture with painted green finishes. The hue also coordinates well with the room's green woodwork.

CENTERPIECE
Positioned on either end of the dining table, Victorian garden urns make dramatic vases. Silver candelabrum and a row of small pumpkins complete the arrangement. Seasonal fruits can stand in for the autumn gourds; consider lemons, green apples, or sculptural pomegranates.

ABOVE: Bare floors show off the kitchen table's turned legs and the architectural lines of the celadon-tinged stepladder. The owners like to move tables out to the lawn whenever possible to dine al fresco.

ABOVE AND OPPOSITE: While the first floor of the house showcases a fresh take on formal interiors, the upstairs bedrooms possess a more whimsical air. Maple headboards from the eighteenth century give a dormered guest room a sense of grandeur; the quirkiness of the short canopies appealed to the homeowners (above). Although the patterns of the antique quilts don't match, their similar green-and-white color schemes help them work well together in this setting. A collection of objects with an equine theme—sculptures, paintings, and wooden yokes among them—reveals the owners' love of horses and all that pertains to them. Outfitted with an antique iron bed frame, a sunny landing accommodates overnight guests and anyone simply in need of a little shut-eye (opposite, above left). The bed also acts as a spot to display the couple's country quilts, and they rotate their many designs from time to time. In bedrooms that lack closets, antique cupboards and armoires provide the necessary storage space (opposite, above right). The freestanding English tub has a romantic air. The wainscoting is stripped and flecked with remnants of yellow and white paint and the floorboards are salvaged pine (opposite, below).

ABOVE: In the parlor, antique rush-seat chairs surround a tavern table the owner modeled after an eighteenth-century design. A reproduction swan decoy based on an old version tops a stenciled blanket chest that he built after a Pennsylvania original from Revolutionary days. A collection of miniature baskets lines the mantel; the primitive-style portraits on the wall were painted by a contemporary artist. The woven rug keeps the overall look of the room simple and unassuming.

One man's appreciation for Early American antiques inspired him to start a business making fine reproductions based on historical designs. The stone farmhouse he shares with his wife is a calling card of sorts, furnished with a combination of period pieces and his own creations. The Pennsylvania house was built in 1790, and as an antique itself, it, too, benefited from the owner's skilled hand.

To expand the interior, a log cabin constructed about 1720 was attached to the main house. The addition now houses the kitchen, laundry room, and a half bath. Throughout much of the main structure, white walls and putty-colored woodwork give the rooms a consistent look and allow the furnishings to take center stage. Much of the pottery, painted finishes, and other decorative details around the house are the work of fellow craftspeople, highly skilled men and women who are equally enchanted with the past.

The owner used salvaged lumber to craft the dining room's plank-top table and fan-back Windsor chairs. The table's graceful turned legs were based on those of an early-1700s farm table the owner admired at a friend's house. A mixture of old and new furnishings populates the kitchen. The dining table, unmatched side chairs, and hall table all date to the nineteenth century. The owner built a hutch to store groceries and a sawbuck table for a workstation.

The bedrooms are serene sanctuaries, layered with the welcoming textures of old wood and soft textiles. Amish and Mennonite quilts, including an 1880 Log Cabin and a red-and-green Oak Leaf variation add color to the master bedroom. In the guest room, sage-green woodwork is a change from most of the rooms in the house, and the bedding in soft shades of green and cream complements the room's overall color scheme. A wooden dowel spanning the length of this cozy retreat supports a linen runner that can be pulled in front of the window when privacy is desired.

ABOVE: The dining room's plank-top table and fan-back Windsors were crafted from salvaged lumber. A local artist painted the canvas floorcloth, drawing inspiration from the traditional Tumbling Block pattern that's also found in classic American quilts. The position of the antique rifle over the mantel continues the old-time farmhouse tradition of positioning the firearm in an easily accessible spot.

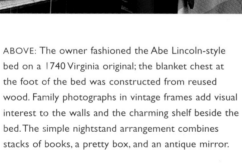

ABOVE: The owner fashioned the Abe Lincoln-style bed on a 1740 Virginia original; the blanket chest at the foot of the bed was constructed from reused wood. Family photographs in vintage frames add visual interest to the walls and the charming shelf beside the bed. The simple nightstand arrangement combines stacks of books, a pretty box, and an antique mirror.

RIGHT: A hand-colored portrait of a couple from the early-1900s watches over the guest room. Touches of sage, cream, and beige create a soft, soothing effect. The deep windowsills throughout the house are ideal spots for a small grouping of objects or a single sculptural piece, like this reproduction candleholder.

Chapter Six

NEW HOMES

THERE ARE A NUMBER OF REASONS A PERSON MIGHT CHOOSE TO BUILD A NEW

HOME THAT CAPTURES THE SPIRIT OF AN OLD FARMHOUSE. AT THE TOP OF THE LIST

IS THE OPPORTUNITY TO COMBINE CLASSIC ARCHITECTURAL STYLING WITH MODERN

AMENITIES. ANOTHER REASON IS THE ABILITY TO SITUATE A NEW RESIDENCE

ANYWHERE, WHETHER ON AN EMPTY LOT IN A SMALL TOWN OR AMID A MAPLE

GROVE ON 100 ACRES. DETAILS ARE THE KEY TO SUCCESS; GABLES, CLAPBOARD

SIDING, AND SALVAGED SHUTTERS CAN AUTHENTICATE AN EXTERIOR WHILE EXPOSED

BEAMS AND GLASS-FRONT CUPBOARDS DO THE SAME INDOORS. THE FOUR HOMES

FEATURED IN THIS CHAPTER (INCLUDING TWO FROM *COUNTRY LIVING*'S POPULAR

ANNUAL FEATURE, OUR "HOUSE OF THE YEAR") PROVE THAT IT REALLY IS POSSIBLE

TO HAVE THE BEST OF BOTH WORLDS.

A DREAM EVOLVES

When a Toronto couple decided to buy a 100-acre horse and cattle farm in eastern Canada, they dreamed of building a weekend getaway that would appear as if it had stood on the property for a century. To accomplish this, they erected a main house from locally quarried stone, attached a red barn-like structure similar to one known to have existed on the farm in 1904, and attached another stuccoed section for the master bedroom. The diverse cluster of connected buildings came to look just as though one family had been adding to the home over the years as space was needed. So pleased were the owners with the completed project, they decided to stay in the country year-round.

Period details bring the same authenticity to the interior: old wooden barn beams, wide plank floors, and thoughtfully placed antiques, to name a few. One thing that has been updated is the arrangement of rooms. By and large, old farmhouses are composed of many small rooms. Here, the sunny sitting area, dining area, and kitchen are all part of one open space. A sisal rug over the tiled floor defines the sitting area where yellow checked slipcovers and striped curtains set a casual and cheerful tone. Locally made wooden chairs surround an antique French table in the dining area. The warm glow of an old lantern suspended above the table encourages guests to linger over their meal.

The kitchen is full of old-fashioned details, from the glass-front cabinets to the reclaimed wood beams that frame the cooking area. A large worktable is positioned between the stove and the dining area, creating a subtle distinction between the two places. A 1930s Hoosier cabinet in the hallway just outside the kitchen stores a collection of antique pewter. To get the look they wanted, the owners painted the cabinet sage green and added new drawer pulls and cabinet knobs.

Soft shades of white and cream on walls, curtains, and furnishings create a restful atmosphere in the home's three bedrooms. Color is introduced through antique and contemporary quilts as well as fresh flowers whenever the garden (or market) allows. Salvaged wood beams punctuate the master bedroom's soaring ceiling. Old wood is also set into the walls above the windows in a guest room where a whitewashed vintage pine dresser stands between a pair of new twin beds.

ABOVE: The sunroom, dining area, and kitchen are all one big space. Yellow checked slipcovers and striped curtains keep the mood casual. The table is an antique from France, while the chairs are locally made.

OPPOSITE: New pulls and paint were added to the 1930s Hoosier cabinet that holds a pewter collection. The kitchen's wide plank floors contrast with the antique terra-cotta tiles in the entryway.

A CLOSER LOOK

EXPOSED BEAMS

Reused wood beams from an old barn frame the kitchen's cooking area. The notched and knotty surface adds texture and height to the space and offers a tangible link between the homeowners and the time when the beams were hewn by hand.

CABINETS

A common sight in country kitchens, glass-front cabinets allowed a homemaker to display both prized possessions and everyday wares. Here, mixing bowls add a dash of color to the room; glassware gleams in a larger cupboard nearby.

WORKTABLE

A custom-made cherry worktable is topped with maple and fitted with vintage-style drawer pulls. The distressed surface complements the old wood of the beams. A five-tiered tray keeps fresh ingredients close at hand.

TILING

Decorative tiling above the stove depicts a cow, a nod to the property's history as a dairy and cattle farm. Brown trim frames the cow and the graphic patterns that flank it, emphasizing its separation from the white backsplash.

ABOVE: The walls in this bedroom were waxed to give them the appearance of age. An old pine dresser was painted white to match the new beds. Coordinated bedding, a blue vase, and a hand-painted vintage luggage stand add cheerful hues to the scene.

ARCHITECTURAL DETAILS

The simplicity of Shaker design had always appealed to the owners of this western Massachusetts residence, so it's no wonder they strove to incorporate Shaker-inspired details in their new home. From a distance, the simple lines and white clapboard siding of the two buildings resemble the region's older farmhouses; the barn's rough-hewn granite columns were copied from similar examples in a machine shop in nearby Hancock Shaker Village. The home's interior is as open and airy as a spacious barn, but period touches sprinkled throughout recall the classic architectural elements of a traditional compartmented farmhouse.

When describing their dream house to their architect, one of the main desires the owners voiced was to have a great room that combined living, dining, and kitchen areas. The dream became a reality. Wooden trusses emphasize the height of the room's vaulted ceiling. In the living area, an unusual fireplace design affords uninterrupted views of the surrounding countryside. Plush sofas covered in soft sky-blue fabric and a brown leather armchair provide ample seating for lively gatherings of family and friends. The woven rug and graphic quilt draped over the arm of a sofa add understated pattern to the setting. Open shelves against the far wall hold a collection of folk art whirligigs.

Butter-yellow paint distinguishes the part of the room devoted to cooking and dining. The same hue can be found on the front of the kitchen drawers. Sage green was chosen for the glass-front cupboards on either side of the room. One of the cupboards features mail-sorting cubbies. The work surface, wall phone, and space for a stool underneath creates an impromptu home office. Shaker-style details in this part of the room include ladder-back chairs with tape seats and shawl rails, a tapered-leg farmhouse table, and minimally ornamented drawers. Beaded-board paneling installed here as well as on the cabinets flanking the fireplace is another nod to the past. Soapstone and maple form the surface of the two-tiered kitchen island. The microwave is tucked below the counter beside the stove to free up surface space for food preparation. The decorative details, which include an old-fashioned kitchen scale, a mustard-painted stepstool, and a pair of garden urns-turned-flower vases further connect the interior with the design of long ago.

LEFT: The owners wanted one large room for cooking, dining, and relaxing—something of a cross between a loft and a medieval dining hall. The airiness and shape of the great room brings to mind a renovated barn. Wood trusses lead the eye up to the vaulted ceiling.

OPPOSITE: The four-foot-high built-in cabinet surrounds the fireplace and conceals a television. The vaulted space with its plush seating is ideal for gatherings of friends and family. Large floor-to-ceiling double-hung windows frame a favorite focal point: a radio tower on a distant hill.

ABOVE AND OPPOSITE: The kitchen abounds with Shaker-inspired details, such as the ladder-back chairs with tape seats and shawl rails and the minimally ornamented drawers. The galley area maximizes efficiency. The deep porcelain sink is in keeping with the barn-like style of the house. The pale colors seem drawn from a sun-washed summer day: whites and off-whites, creamy yellows, and the palest of greens. Sunlight pours into the area from windows on three sides.

THE SPIRIT OF THE PAST

To produce our House of the Year, the editors of *Country Living* attend home-building shows, furniture markets, and antiques fairs all around the country, gathering information on the latest building materials, home furnishings, and collecting trends. Next, we create a wish list that reflects the concerns of our readers—people who appreciate the traditions of the past yet want to make the most of today's conveniences. The charming farmhouse pictured on these pages is a fresh take on the ever-popular Greek Revival style, combining classic exterior elements (porch, cupola, clapboard siding) with a Douglas fir post-and-beam construction. Indoors, exposed beams join period details such as old growth, heart-pine flooring, beaded-board paneling, and craftsman-style banisters. The cupola features motorized windows for ventilation.

Just inside the front door, exposed beams and pine flooring envelope the open living/dining area in warm wood tones. A vaulted ceiling in the living area adds a sense of drama to the cozy setting. The tiled fireplace surround exhibits a palette of soft tans and browns. At the windows, curtain rods carved in a spiral shape and drapes with a zigzag trim add texture to the scene.

A roomy country kitchen tops the list of priorities for most homeowners today. This kitchen captures the look on a grand scale. A double-height trussed ceiling over the generous cooking area enhances the room's spacious proportions. The end of the kitchen opens out into a sitting area, where dinner guests can gather to converse before the meal without the cook feeling left out. French doors lead out to a deck that overlooks the garden.

Four restful bedrooms fill out the house, with three located on the second story and a romantic master suite on the first floor. The ever-popular color scheme of blue and white was chosen for the master bedroom. The soft ocean hues complement the honey-toned timber framing. Blue is even used on the floor, where square tiles are a lighthearted change from the pine floorboards found elsewhere in the house.

ABOVE: In the living room, narrow red-and-white striped fabric reminiscent of mattress ticking was chosen for the sofa, a plush armchair, and an ottoman that functions as a coffee table. On the floor, a woven carpet continues the striped motif in a deeper red hue. A pair of antique garden urns flanks a horizontal Victorian flower still life on the high mantel. A sturdy basket placed beside the sofa provides attractive storage for magazines, throws, games, and sewing supplies.

OPPOSITE: The lower ceiling in the dining area creates a sense of intimacy that is well suited to entertaining. Upholstered slipper chairs and an antiqued white table base complement the room's white walls and draperies. Note the spiral detailing on the table base that mirrors the decorative curtain rods. A shelving unit open in front and back displays a collection of nineteenth-century yellowware bowls whose placement is kept airy. Striped red-and-white rugs identical to those in the living area link the two spaces.

ABOVE: A double-height wood-trussed ceiling over the spacious cooking area enhances the large proportions of the kitchen. Details reflect timeless tradition: the beaded-board backsplash, soapstone countertops, glass-sided cabinets, and open shelves for everyday wares. The shelves are supported by custom brackets. In this kind of setting, even stainless steel appliances take on an old-fashioned air.

A CLOSER LOOK

SINKS

In the master bath, two full-size sinks are housed in a farmhouse-style table with three drawers. The deep shelf holds towels and grooming essentials. Brass hardware complements the lighting fixture on the wall and the tub's handheld showerhead.

CABINET

A custom-built, glass-front cabinet stores towels and bath products. Fish-shaped hinges add a whimsical touch to this traditional-looking piece. Towels can provide an extra splash of color in a bath, like the soft green and lavender seen here.

BEADED BOARD

Beaded board coats the lower portion of the walls and the front of the tub. Painted powder blue, the paneling continues the blue-and-white color scheme from the master bedroom. White beaded board below a colorful wall is another classic country look.

FLOOR

Small, octagonal floor tiles were a common sight in bathrooms a century ago; this black-and-white pattern, available through most home-improvement stores, still looks fresh today. A bath mat hangs over the shower door handle when not in use.

SIDE CHAIR

An old wooden side chair can be an essential accessory in a bathroom. Positioned beside the tub, it stands at the ready to hold bath towels, robes, books, or a refreshing drink. The worn finish on this chair pairs well with the look of the room.

A QUIRKY CHARACTER

The husband-and-wife architecture team that designed this stone farmhouse for *Country Living*'s annual feature, House of the Year, makes a living building new homes based on historic structures. Rather than copying an old house board for board, the dwellings serve as starting points for fresh interpretations. Elements are borrowed: proportions, materials, window size, and roof pitch, to name a few. The residence shown on these pages drew inspiration from the eighteenth-century stone farmhouses that dot the Lancaster County, Pennsylvania, countryside. The siding materials include a six-inch veneer of blue and brown Seneca limestone. A roof of saw-cut cedar shingles, copper gutters and downspouts, and operable shutters painted a warm red complete the vernacular look.

Cocoa-brown walls and drapery give the living room a sophisticated air. Sisal carpeting, off-white upholstery, and glossy white paint on molding and mantel add to the room's formal feeling, and the reproduction furniture achieves an authentic, period look. Technology from the twenty-first century is hidden within the wood-burning fireplace: a gas starter that warms things up quickly without any need for kindling. Brown walls and white trim are also used in the dining room, although in this setting the wainscoting is painted white as well. Sisal carpeting and draperies similar to the living room's further unify the two spaces. A pair of salvaged columns flanks the floor-to-ceiling mantel to dramatic effect.

Overhead beams lend the kitchen the feeling of an old-fashioned farmhouse, as do a wide apron-front sink and built-in cabinets that resemble antique cupboards. The mix of built-in and freestanding storage supports the illusion that this is an old kitchen whose furniture was accumulated over many years. Vintage-style lighting over the island provides an illuminating finishing touch; additional lights are recessed into the ceiling.

The master bedroom's bold color scheme combines sunny yellow fabrics with deep violet walls. Above the bed, a descending canopy of mosquito netting recalls the nineteenth-century French Colonial style. The bedroom's purple walls continue in the master bath where eye-level wainscoting is painted bright white. On the floor, limestone tiles are edged in a basket-weave pattern of black and white marble.

ABOVE: In the great room, cocoa-brown walls and glossy white paint on the moldings give the room a sophisticated and formal air. Cherry-red accents appear throughout, including layered textiles and throw pillows on the sofas, lampshades, and a glittering collection of beaded fruit in a tall glass jar. By mixing period reproductions—plump sofas with ball-and-claw feet—with modern accent pieces such as the quirky, elongated lampshades—the room retains its formality but is nonetheless inviting and comfortable. A group of framed prints adorns the mantel.

ABOVE: Five brown-and-white transferware plates, each with an accompanying mercury glass vase, stand above the fireplace, mirroring the living room's mantel-top arrangement. An elegant etched-glass mirror from the early 1900s looks down on the table and chairs, also reproductions that impart an antique look. Overhead, pillar candles set on a circular chandelier cast a warm glow on the scene.

LEFT AND BELOW: The romance of the master bedroom is accentuated by its French design influences, including a curvy recamier and a white dresser with a decorative painted finish. The bed skirt and upholstered headboard repeat the fabric used for draperies. The deeply ruffled duvet and pillow sham are reminiscent of a ball gown's petticoat. Framed fashion illustrations from the early 1900s inspired the rows of ruffles on the duvet and pillow sham.

OPPOSITE: The beamed ceiling lends the kitchen the feeling of an old-fashioned farmhouse as does the design of the built-in cabinets. A cherry-topped island with beaded-board paneling on the side features ample work space up top and deep drawers below. The windows extend from the counter to the ceiling, allowing sunlight to stream in.

PHOTOGRAPHY CREDITS

Page 2: Keith Scott Morton; Page 6: Michael Luppino; Page 8: Keith Scott Morton; Page 10: Keith Scott Morton; Page 12: William P. Steele; Page 14: Keith Scott Morton; Page 16: Keith Scott Morton; Page 17 (top): Keith Scott Morton; Page 17 (bottom): Keith Scott Morton; Page 18: Keith Scott Morton; Page 19: Keith Scott Morton; Page 20: William P. Steele; Page 22: William P. Steele; Page 23: William P. Steele; Page 24: William P. Steele; Page 25: William P. Steele; Page 26: William P. Steele; Page 27: Gridley & Graves; Page 28: Gridley & Graves; Page 30: Gridley & Graves; Page 31: Gridley & Graves; Page 32: Gridley & Graves; Page 33: Gridley & Graves; Page 34: Michael Luppino; Page 36: Michael Luppino; Page 37 (left): Michael Luppino; Page 37 (right): Michael Luppino; Page 38: Michael Luppino; Page 39: Michael Luppino; Page 40: Michael Luppino; Page 41: Michael Luppino; Page 42: Gridley & Graves; Page 44: Gridley & Graves; Page 45: Gridley & Graves; Page 46: Gridley & Graves; Page 47: Gridley & Graves; Page 48: Keith Scott Morton; Page 50: Keith Scott Morton; Page 52: Keith Scott Morton; Page 53: Keith Scott Morton; Page 54: Keith Scott Morton; Page 55: Keith Scott Morton; Page 56: Keith Scott Morton; Page 58: Keith Scott Morton; Page 59: Keith Scott Morton; Page 60: Keith Scott Morton; Page 61: Keith Scott Morton; Page 62: Keith Scott Morton; Page 64: Keith Scott Morton; Page 65: Keith Scott Morton; Page 66: Keith Scott Morton; Page 67: Keith Scott Morton; Page 68: Keith Scott Morton; Page 70: Keith Scott Morton; Page 71: Keith Scott Morton; Page 72: Keith Scott Morton; Page 73: Keith Scott Morton; Page 74: Keith Scott Morton; Page 75: Keith Scott Morton; Page 76: Keith Scott Morton; Page 78: Michael Luppino; Page 80: Michael Luppino; Page 81: Michael Luppino; Page 82: Michael Luppino; Page 83: Keith Scott Morton; Page 84: Michael Luppino; Page 85: Michael Luppino; Page 86: Keith Scott Morton; Page 88: Keith Scott Morton; Page 89: Keith Scott Morton; Page 90: Keith Scott Morton; Page 91: Keith Scott Morton; Page 92: Keith Scott Morton; Page 93: Keith Scott Morton; Page 94: Michael Luppino; Page 96: Michael Luppino; Page 97: Michael Luppino; Page 98: Michael Luppino; Page 99 (top): Michael Luppino; Page 99 (bottom): Michael Luppino; Page 100: Michael Luppino; Page 101: Michael Luppino; Page 102: Steven Randazzo; Page 104: Steven Randazzo; Page 105 (top): Steven Randazzo; Page 105 (bottom): Steven Randazzo; Page 106: Steven Randazzo; Page 107: Steven Randazzo; Page 108: Steven Randazzo; Page 109: Steven Randazzo; Page 110: Keith Scott Morton; Page 112: Keith Scott Morton; Page 114: Keith Scott Morton; Page 115: Keith Scott Morton; Page 116: Keith Scott Morton; Page 117: Keith Scott Morton; Page 118: Steven Randazzo; Page 120: Steven Randazzo; Page 121 (left): Steven Randazzo; Page 121 (right): Steven Randazzo; Page 122: Steven Randazzo; Page 123: Steven Randazzo; Page 124: Gridley & Graves; Page 126 (top): Gridley & Graves; Page 126 (bottom): Gridley & Graves; Page 127: Gridley & Graves; Page 128: John Coolidge; Page 129: Gridley & Graves; Page 130: Keith Scott Morton; Page 132: Keith Scott Morton; Page 133 (left): Keith Scott Morton; Page 133 (right): Keith Scott Morton; Page 134: Keith Scott Morton; Page 135: Keith Scott Morton; Page 136: Keith Scott Morton; Page 138: Keith Scott Morton; Page 140: Keith Scott Morton; Page 141: Keith Scott Morton; Page 142: Keith Scott Morton; Page 143 (left): Keith Scott Morton; Page 143 (right): Keith Scott Morton; Page 144: Keith Scott Morton; Page 146: Keith Scott Morton; Page 147: Keith Scott Morton; Page 148: Keith Scott Morton; Page 149: Keith Scott Morton; Page 150: Keith Scott Morton; Page 151: Keith Scott Morton; Page 152: Chuck Baker; Page 154: Chuck Baker; Page 155: Chuck Baker; Page 156: Chuck Baker; Page 157: Chuck Baker; Page 158: Chuck Baker; Page 159 (top left): Chuck Baker; Page 159 (top right): Chuck Baker; Page 159 (bottom): Chuck Baker; Page 160: John Blais; Page 162: John Blais; Page 163 (left): John Blais; Page 163 (right): John Blais; Page 164: William P. Steele; Page 166: Robin Stubbert; Page 168: Robin Stubbert; Page 169: Robin Stubbert; Page 170: Robin Stubbert; Page 171: Robin Stubbert; Page 172: William P. Steele; Page 174: William P. Steele; Page 175: William P. Steele; Page 176: William P. Steele; Page 177: William P. Steele; Page 178: Keith Scott Morton; Page 180: Keith Scott Morton; Page 181: Keith Scott Morton; Page 182: Keith Scott Morton; Page 183: Keith Scott Morton; Page 184: Keith Scott Morton; Page 186: Keith Scott Morton; Page 187: Keith Scott Morton; Page 188: Keith Scott Morton; Page 189 (left): Keith Scott Morton; Page 189 (right): Keith Scott Morton

INDEX